BY BOB HARPER

Skinny Meals

The Skinny Rules

Jumpstart to Skinny

Are You Ready?

SKINNY MEALS

SKINNY MEALS

*Everything You Need
to Lose Weight—Fast!*

BOB HARPER

Photos by Kelly Campbell

BALLANTINE BOOKS TRADE PAPERBACKS
NEW YORK

This book proposes a program of dietary and nutrition recommendations for the reader to follow. No book, however, can replace the diagnostic and medical expertise of a qualified physician. Please consult your doctor (and, if you are pregnant, your ob/gyn) before making sustained or extensive changes in your diet, particularly if you suffer from any diagnosed medical condition or have any symptoms that may require treatment.

A Ballantine Books Trade Paperback Original

Published in the United States by Ballantine Books, an imprint of Random House, a division of Random House LLC, New York, a Penguin Random House Company.

BALLANTINE and the HOUSE colophon are registered trademarks of Random House LLC.

LIBRARY OF CONGRESS CATALOGING-IN-PUBLICATION DATA
Harper, Bob.
Skinny meals : everything you need to lose weight—fast! / Bob Harper ; photos by Kelly Campbell.
pages cm
Includes index.
ISBN 978-0-804-17889-1
eBook ISBN 978-0-804-17860-0
1. Weight loss. 2. Reducing diets—Recipes. 3. Reducing exercises.
I. Title.
RM222.2.H245 2014
613.2'5—dc23   2014001423

Printed in the United States of America on acid-free paper

Photos by Kelly Campbell

Photo styling by Roscoe Betsill

www.ballantinebooks.com

246897531

CONTENTS

LEAN LUNCHES

THINNER DINNERS

HAPPY SNACKING

PART III

SKINNY TOOLS: SHOP, PREPARE, EAT!

INTRODUCTION: WELCOME TO SKINNY EATING

Have you ever read about some celebrity's dramatic weight loss and thought how much easier dropping pounds would be if you had the support of a personal chef like so many famous people do? Ever imagined the ease of having someone tell you exactly what to put in your mouth, and when (not to mention shopping and preparing all your food each day)?

Well, unless you go hire yourself a live-in chef (cha-ching) or buy a subscription to a frozen-meal delivery service (bland, yuck), this book is as close as you can get to that experience. I'll be your kitchen wizard and motivator, giving you one hundred amazing options for meals that are easy to cook and deliciously satisfying—and that will promote *fast weight loss*. I've made recommendations so you can easily put meals together for a month's worth of menus, and I've even given you week-by-week shopping lists—order from one of those popular grocery delivery services and you won't even have to do the shopping yourself! Don't you feel like a celebrity already?

More good news: every *Skinny Meals* recipe adheres to the nonnegotiable rules for getting to thin that I set out in my book *The Skinny Rules*. This means that each is rules-abiding in terms of what should go into every meal, and what amounts and kinds of ingredients (protein, carbs, fiber, sodium, etc.), and when. When you eat exclusively from the recipes in this book (or combine them with recipes from *The Skinny Rules* to give yourself the most possible options), you will be living by my rules for overall daily calories (no recipe in this book has more than 330 calories!), protein, carbs, fiber, sodium, fruits, vegetables, and water.

What does all this mean to you in the short term? No more standing in front of the fridge wondering what on earth you should make (and finally saying "the hell with it" and ordering a massive pizza for delivery). No more calorie counting and worrying about macronutrient combinations (carbs and protein and fat, oh my!). No more confusion! Whether you create your own daily menu combinations or follow the ones I've supplied, I'll make grabbing breakfast on the fly, packing lunch for the office, snacking, and assembling dinner in a rush much, much easier. Automated, even. And automation is your friend when you are trying to get rid of bad eating habits and adopt better ones.

Automated, however, doesn't mean joyless. It doesn't mean nasty, cardboard-y food. It doesn't mean denying yourself the flavors of the world. My Skinny Meals draw inspiration from Thailand to Louisiana, Hawaii to France, and the Mediterranean to Mexico. Because although having fewer decisions to make around meal prep will help you meet your weight-loss goals, having diverse flavors—all "skinnified" for your eating pleasure—will make life so much more colorful. Some of the food in these pages is so scrumptious that you could entertain guests in style without breaking your skinny stride (though obviously you'll want to multiply the amount of ingredients by the number of people you'll be serving!).

With twenty breakfast options, thirty-five lunches, thirty-five dinners, and ten snack recipes, you could mix and match for months and never get bored using my Skinny Meals. I hope you'll try any and all that seem even remotely appetizing to you—the more go-to recipes you can develop, the better. Each Skinny Meal recipe you love is one more powerful weapon in your battle against the bulge.

Here's to your successful weight loss!

PART I

SKINNY
RULES
FOR
LIFE

THE SKINNY RULES RECAP:
THE NONNEGOTIABLE PRINCIPLES
FOR GETTING TO THIN

From when to eat protein to how much fiber, how to cut back on sodium, and how to "splurge," my Skinny Rules are still and always will be your foolproof road map to getting to your healthy weight. They are the rules I teach my private clients and the guidelines I try to pound into the heads of the contestants on *The Biggest Loser* each season. I know they work. I've seen them put to weight-loss action!

The science behind why each of the following rules will help you lose weight is explained fully in *The Skinny Rules;* what follows is a summary to refresh your memory or get you started.

RULE 1:   DRINK A LARGE GLASS OF WATER BEFORE
           EVERY MEAL—NO EXCUSES!

Most of us are chronically underhydrated. That doesn't mean we're completely dehydrated and panting for water—you'd know it if that were the case. But underhydrated is perhaps even worse because it's something you are likely not aware of . . . you're just going about your day, slightly parched and too often quenching your thirst with a soda, juice, or coffee shop concoction—none of which is what you need.

Above and beyond its ability to quench your thirst noncalorically, water has three primary weight-loss benefits: it keeps food moving through the system, it makes you feel full, and it increases your "resting energy expenditure," which is your body's rate of calorie burning while you're doing nothing but sitting around. If you work out much at all (which you should), water also keeps your organs healthy while you're sweating and will help you recuperate faster.

This is such a simple weight-loss rule, people. You simply must make drinking water a habit—it's perhaps the easiest thing I'm asking you to do.

In the menus for *The Skinny Rules,* I added "H₂Ox2" to every meal because I wanted you to drink two standard-size glasses of water (each about 8 ounces, so 16 ounces in all). I've done the same in my *Skinny Meals* menus, so you'll be drinking water with breakfast, lunch, dinner, and snacks. You can also drink coffee (ideally without milk, but go lowfat if you must have dairy), green tea, or seltzer with your meals, but also have water at every meal—that's the only way to get enough throughout the day.

Here's a tip to help you get into this habit: put a tall glass of water by your bedside every night. That way, it'll be there for you in the morning. Chug it down the moment you first throw your legs over the side of the bed—an excellent way to start your day!

RULE 2:   DON'T DRINK YOUR CALORIES

Drinking water—as I describe in Rule 1—is not "drinking your calories." Drinking your calories refers to the tendency too many people have to quench their thirst with caloric and/or sugary drinks—sodas, juices, or hot concoctions with whipped cream and caramel drizzled on top (please, oh please, stop ordering your hot drinks with whole milk or flavorings or toppings). This is a recipe for disaster, because sugar drives up your blood sugar, which tells the pancreas to make more insulin, which makes you hungry, which makes you want to eat. Binge time!

If you're a full-calorie soda drinker, you're guzzling empty calories. If you're a zero-calorie soda drinker, don't pat yourself on the back just yet. Why? The artificial sweeteners that replace the actual sugar or high-fructose corn syrup only serve to keep you attuned to and craving unnaturally sweet things.

You think fruit juice is a better option? Think again! If you want fruit, eat fruit. The whole thing, so you get the fiber in its skin as well. And sports drinks? Don't even get me started! Clever marketing, I'll grant you: put the word "sports" in the name and people somehow associate the product with exercise and make the leap to drinking the stuff without having exercised. And the ounce load?! Most sports drinks come in those massive 20-ounce bottles—the equivalent, in most cases, of a 12-ounce full-sugar soda (without the bubbles). See above for why that's bad!

Alcohol? There's a place for it when you've reached your goal weight. A glass of red wine has some health benefits because grapes contain polyphenols, and polyphenols are good. Hard liquor—no polyphenols, people. Beer? Can you say "carb load"?! And don't let's forget that when you drink alcohol—more than just a glass of red for dinner—you often relax your vigilance, you loosen up your resolve to lose weight . . . you pig out. Stop the madness!

Bottom line: break your calories-in-a-cup habit and switch to seltzer water (with a lemon or lime for flavor), black coffee, or green tea (hot or cold) and . . . water!

RULE 3: EAT PROTEIN AT EVERY MEAL—
OR STAY HUNGRY AND GROUCHY

Protein satisfies hunger and keeps you feeling full longer than the other nutritional categories of food. So, it's pretty simple: if you eat it at every meal, you will be spreading out those hunger-reducing benefits over the course of the day.

But I also want you to eat protein at every meal because it would be impossible to consume your daily quota all in one sitting; you'll need to spread your protein consumption over the course of the day to make sure you get enough overall.

My rule of thumb about how much protein to eat per day is to take your weight and divide it by 2. That's how many grams of protein you should get each day. If you weigh 200 pounds, that's 100 grams of protein. My recipes will help you get up there, though on your meatless day you'll have to work a little harder. My rule of thumb isn't completely scientific, but it's the calculation that works for me, my clients, my contestants. And more and more scientific research shows that a high-protein diet with limited carbs results in better weight control. Which is what you want, right?

Eating some kind of protein—from eggs to meat to fish to hard cheese and non-animal proteins—at every meal gives you an amazing variety of options and will therefore keep your diet diverse and interesting (not a rule, but a good idea nonetheless). That said, take a look at the breakdown of the hundred recipes in this book and you'll see a pattern: eggs (and especially egg whites) and fish are my personal go-to proteins and the ones I suggest you rely on most heavily as well. Eggs are naturally low calorie (an egg white has only 20 calories; the yolk adds another 60 calories) and are incredibly versatile. They make everything taste richer. Fish contains omega-3 fatty acids (so do eggs, and some have more added—look for those), which are linked to the prevention of a number of chronic diseases. But then there's the simple fact that a serving of eggs or fish will always be bigger than the same-ounce serving of a heavier protein, like beef. That means more on your plate—more bites, more satisfaction. And less fat!

It's not that I discourage you from eating poultry or beef or even pork; chicken and turkey and lean beef are on display in my Skinny Meals. And though I myself am not a fan of "the other white meat," I've included one pork recipe. My overriding advice, however, is to buy organic, grass-fed meats and organic, free-range poultry if you can. You'll be getting cleaner, tastier meats, and taste matters when you are trying to lose weight!

See Rule 12 for my thinking on non-animal proteins.

RULE 4:   SLASH YOUR INTAKE OF REFINED FLOURS AND GRAINS

A "refined" version of anything sounds fancier and purer, doesn't it? Well, when it comes to flours and grains, the refining process is only fancy in its terminology: it's the process for stripping out nutritional value. That's not more pure at all. In fact, that's toxic to your weight loss!

The refining process removes bran and germ from grains. You end up with products that are smoother and lighter (in both color and density) but are also now devoid of the digestive help that bran gives you and the vitamins and minerals in the germ. You are left with starchy carbs, which actually depress important hormones that cause you to feel full and stimulate hormones that make you feel hungry. How can that combination help you lose weight? It can't!

Many people feel that this rule takes some getting used to, but if you cook from *Skinny Meals* (or from the recipes in *The Skinny Rules*), you'll quickly move away from anything refined and, when appropriate (see Rule 7), toward whole grains like whole-grain pasta, quinoa, barley, and farro. And that's the operative word, the one thing you need to be vigilant about as you make this switch: stick to whole grains and nothing but whole grains.

If the nutritional information on a product (bread, pasta, etc.) does not lead with the words "whole-grain wheat flour" or "sprouted whole wheat," walk right on by! Ignore any and all marketing ploys that suggest something is "natural" or "whole wheat," because those terms are not the same as "whole grain."

As a practical matter, this means you're going to buy only "whole-grain" bread (like Ezekiel products) and pasta and, as you'll see in the pantry-stocking section, you're going to donate or throw out everything else.

RULE 5: EAT 30 TO 50 GRAMS OF FIBER A DAY

Most people don't get enough fiber in their diets, though supplement marketers seem to have convinced too many that a spoonful of stir-in fiber will help make up that shortfall. No! I want you to *eat* enough fiber, not stir something manufactured into water and call it a day.

There are two kinds of fiber—soluble and insoluble. Soluble fiber is what you get in the mix-in supplements (in nature, it's found in fruits, veggies, beans, nuts, bran, barley, and flax). It gets absorbed into the bloodstream and performs many important health functions thereafter. But the nonsoluble kind of fiber—also found in brans, the skins of fruits and vegetables, nuts and seeds—is what I want you to focus on here.

Let me state this plainly: eat fiber, lose weight. It's vital to your digestive system in that it helps "sweep" your gastrointestinal tract, but, like protein, it also improves your "satiety signals" and sense of fullness.

If you eat according to my menus, you will get between 30 and 35 grams of fiber a day, which is good (and much better than what you've likely been eating, I can promise you), but you can always eat more berries or vegetables to improve on that number. Add the following to any meal and do the math:

FOOD	FIBER
1/2 cup mixed berries	= 4 grams
1/2 cup raspberries	= 4 grams
1/2 cup blueberries	= 2 grams
1/2 cup strawberries	= 2 grams
1/2 cup blackberries	= 4 grams
1 cup zucchini	= 8 grams
1 cup spinach	= 7 grams
1 cup cabbage	= 5 grams
1 cup Brussels sprouts	= 4 grams

RULE 6: EAT APPLES AND BERRIES EVERY SINGLE DAY. EVERY. SINGLE. DAY!

Your berries don't have to be fresh. Sometimes they won't be in season (meaning the ones at the market will be very expensive) and sometimes they won't look too fresh even if they are a good deal (and they're not a good deal if they are two days away from compost!). Go ahead and buy frozen berries to add as is to smoothies, or thaw them out and mix them into yogurt. Just be sure that your frozen berries contain nothing else. No added sugar, no added "fruit juice," please!

Rule 5 taught you that berries are high in fiber, which you now know is a key to weight loss. Apples are also high-fiber—4 grams for an average-size apple. Both are also low in calories, so get with the program and add some berries and an apple to your diet every single day. Yes—you heard me right—this rule isn't about taking anything out of your diet but is instead about *adding* foods to your plate. You'll be doing yourself a fiber favor and getting a nice dose of natural sweetness at the same time.

Need more reasons to live by this rule? Well, above and beyond fiber and sweetness, berries and apples have something else going for them: their colorful skins are high in a class of molecules called phytochemicals. From metabolism to skin health to gut (digestive tract) health, let's just say that phytochemicals are a good, good thing.

You'll see that many of my breakfast and snack recipes have berries or an apple in the ingredients. Feel free to add them to your own Skinny-Rules-abiding recipes too.

NO CARBS AFTER LUNCH

Don't panic—I'm not making you cut out simple carbs like fruits and vegetables after lunch! Complex carbs are what I'm concerned with here, and what I need you to pledge to forego in your afternoon snack and dinner. As we learned in Rule 2, your body interprets complex carbs as sugar, which cues your pancreas to make more insulin, which triggers appetite. The later in the day you eat a complex carb, the more likely it is that you will get food cravings at night. That never ends well!

This is a rule that most people think is going to be hard to adhere to— what, no pasta or rice or potatoes for dinner, Bob?! But the feedback I get from most Skinny Rulers is that it's actually not a hard rule at all. The trick is to reimagine your likely long-held image of a "complete" dinner. Though you may have been brought up to think that your dinner plate needs a white side dish (like potatoes, pasta, rice, or bread), it really shouldn't have a mound of starchy carbs on it at all. Your dinner plate needs to be lean and green.

Once you start to develop a repertoire of no-complex-carb, go-to meals that you can easily and happily have for dinner (with help from the book you're holding in your hands!), you will realize how very easy it is to eat this way. It's just a shift from what you're used to, that's all. Remember: complex carbs in moderation at breakfast and lunch. Protein, fruit, and vegetables for snacks. And then—say it with me—"lean and green" for dinner.

RULE 8: **LEARN TO READ FOOD LABELS SO YOU KNOW WHAT YOU ARE EATING**

You want to lose weight, you're going to have to be a smarter consumer.

By that I mean smarter about what you put in your mouth and what you buy at the store. You're going to have to learn how to read food labels so you know what foods to bring back to your kitchen in the first place!

In *The Skinny Rules* I outline ingredients to watch out for (not to mention lengthy ingredient lists) and I explain complicated terms like "net carbs," "percentage of daily values," and a number of sinister chemicals. But here's the short course of things to pay attention to.

Serving size and *number of servings per container:* A small serving size or a high number of servings per container will yield smaller amounts of everything listed on the label, which means that food manufacturers often manipulate these two pieces of information in an attempt to fool you into thinking that the food is better for you—lower in calories or higher in protein, for example—than it really is!

Calories: Here's the bottom line: if a food has more than 350 calories per serving (remember to scrutinize the serving info), that's a pretty good sign that it is too calorie-dense and you should look for something else to munch on.

Protein: You now know that if you divide your weight in half you will come up with how much protein you want to eat every day (your weight is in pounds, but your protein needs are in grams), so keep an eye out for foods with enough protein to help you meet that goal. Just a few grams of protein? Not enough.

Sugar and salt: No matter what it's called—from innocent-sounding "honey" and "agave" (which has a place in my pantry, don't get me wrong) to the evil-sounding "high-fructose corn syrup"—if sugar is one of the first five ingredients on the label, put it back on the shelf. It's not for you. As for salt, I want you to keep your sodium intake under 2,000 milligrams a day (see Rule 16). With that in mind, study food labels and you'll see just how quickly you can get to that level if you eat processed foods.

Fat and trans fats: You should get between 25 and 35 percent of your daily calories from healthy fats. Though you can and should stand in the aisle and do the math (based on the serving size, number of servings per container, and how many servings you think you could power down), the handy piece of information on the label is the "percentage of fat calories per serving." If that number is over 20 percent, walk away. And now I'll make this even easier for you: if there is any number for trans fats at all, run!

Carbs: See Rule 4 above—if it doesn't say "100 percent whole-grain flour," you're not having it. "All-natural wheat flour"? No! "Potato starch"? No!

Fiber: You're trying to get between 30 and 50 grams of fiber a day, so stand there and do some math. In combination with other things in your shopping cart, will this food help you achieve that goal?

RULE 9:   STOP GUESSING ABOUT PORTION SIZE
           AND GET IT RIGHT—FOR GOOD

We have been conditioned to think of a massive plate of food as a "good deal" when at a restaurant but, oh, what a terrible deal it usually is for your waistline.

What's needed here is an understanding of what a proper portion looks like on a plate. I mean, consider this: a proper portion of a piece of meat is about 4 ounces, and that's about the size of the palm of your hand. A steak the size of your whole plate? That's enough to feed a family of four (or more) people!

As you learn to cook more for yourself (see Rule 15), you'll gain the needed perspective on what your portion size really should be. In the meantime, I recommend buying foods that come packaged in single portions, like 6-ounce containers of plain nonfat Greek yogurt, 2-ounce bags of raw almonds, or pre-portioned packages of natural peanut or almond butter. Or stock up on the kinds of foods that I urge you to gorge yourself on (i.e., "Harpersizing"): veggies, veggies, veggies; berries, apples, berries!

RULE 10:   NO MORE ADDED SWEETENERS, INCLUDING ARTIFICIAL ONES

An interesting fact: we humans have specialized taste buds that detect sweetness. But don't let that knowledge help you rationalize that we are made to eat sweets. We might have needed more sugar when we were running around all day hunting and gathering for our next meal, but we don't run around all day anymore. Do you even run at all? I didn't think so!

Remember, sugar triggers insulin production, which makes you hungry, which makes you want to eat. Sugar also stimulates the liver to make new fat cells, and once you have a fat cell, you have it forever.

I don't have a problem with eating naturally sweet foods like most fruit and berries, but I don't want you to be eating foods with added sugar (it's in all kinds of products—once you start reading food labels, you'll see it everywhere), and I especially want to break your sweet habit by staying away from artificial sweeteners like aspartame and stevia. It's true that those artificial sweeteners aren't adding fat or calories to your diet, but they *are* feeding your desire for yet more sweet things.

But here's another interesting fact: the less sugar you eat, the less you'll crave it. And if you can break the hold that hypersweet, manufactured food has on you, you'll actually be turned off by that taste the next time you encounter it. All of which is to say: breaking your sugar habit gets easier as you go.

RULE 11: GET RID OF THOSE WHITE POTATOES

Living by the Skinny Rules means that you have to forge some new habits. Rule 7 asks you to stop putting a starchy product on your plate at night, and white potatoes are part of the dinnertime ban. But with white spuds, we need to go one step further: you're going to have to ban them from your daily menus altogether. (See Rule 20, though—you can reintroduce them at one meal a week if you really want to.)

It's not that white potatoes are inherently *bad* for you; rather, it's that they seem to be a food most people can't eat in anything resembling moderation. From potatoes you get French fries, potato chips, mashed potatoes, and hash browns (in their many manufactured shapes and sizes), and none of those preparations is low in fat (each features oil or butter, or both!), and none is ever really served in moderation. Plus, the nutritional value of a white potato is negligible. You can do better! Sweet potatoes are a great and nutritious alternative, and you'll see several Skinny Meals in which they star. Turnips and parsnips roast up nicely, too.

RULE 12: MAKE ONE DAY A WEEK MEATLESS

I'm actually talking animal protein-less here, people. That's meatless, eggless, dairy-less. Above and beyond being positive that this rule will help you lose weight, I also want to push you to think (and cook) outside of your usual comfort zone. It'll be a very good thing to expose yourself to fruits, vegetables, beans, and nuts that you have passed by before. Discover your affinity for spaghetti squash or zucchini or tempeh or garbanzo beans and you will have discovered a new ingredient for your bag of weight-loss tricks!

As you thumb through the recipes in this book, you will likely notice that many of the breakfast options are naturally without animal protein (just stay away from any with eggs or egg whites in the ingredient lists). My Garbanzo Falafel Salad (page 81) and Tempeh Burrito (page 79) are also meatless. Lots of other recipes are easily adaptable to the meatless option by simply replacing the animal protein with beans or tempeh and/or the chicken broth with vegetable broth.

You may also soon realize that I haven't offered any tofu recipes. On meatless days, I prefer tempeh over tofu. Because of the fermentation process used in its creation, tempeh is higher in dietary fiber and vitamins, and is much higher in protein: 8.1 grams per serving for tofu versus 15 grams for tempeh.

You'll see a burst like this on many recipes—this indicates that a meatless protein swap is simple and easy!

RULE 13: GET RID OF FAST FOODS AND FRIED FOODS

There was a time when eating at a fast-food chain was a rare treat because they were costly and the "restaurants" themselves were hard to find (i.e., *not* everywhere on the planet). Now, of course, it's hard for many people to imagine a week (or a day) going by *without* a stop in or a drive-through for some fast food. How dangerously times have changed!

Yes, I said dangerously. There is a long list of medical reasons to stay the heck away from deep-fried, mass-produced, jumbo-sized foods, including inflammation issues like cholesterol and that insulin-production problem you've learned about, associated with sugar and carbs. Greasy fast food is also bad for your skin and can cause diarrhea, bad breath, and heartburn. Need more reasons to stay away from the stuff? How about the fundamental issue we're concerned with here, which can be communicated in this simple equation:

Fried and/or processed fast foods + your mouth = weight gain

Do yourself a major favor and simply keep driving by that fast-food place. If you live by Rule 15—make a good number of your meals for yourself—you'll be planning your shopping and your meals ahead more often, and that will mean fewer opportunities for tempting fast food. Like sugar, the less often you eat fried or fast food, the less desire you'll have for it. Start to break your taste for it today!

RULE 14: EAT A REAL BREAKFAST

One habit that almost all of my contestants on *The Biggest Loser* have in common when they come on the show is that they have been chronic breakfast skippers. Whether that's because they have been trying to diet by cutting out the one meal a day that they don't have much time for, or because they don't really know what constitutes a healthy meal in the land of eggs, bacon, and bread, they've been skipping it, and they've paid dearly. They pay in the form of being absolutely ravenous later in the morning and certainly by lunchtime. Which inevitably leads to eating more than they need (and less nutritiously) at subsequent meals. I see it every time.

I understand that most of us are rushing out the door to get to work and that grabbing something to eat quickly is the best we can do. But that doesn't mean that the "something" has to be a nutritionally barren bagel or a doughnut or a prepared egg sandwich from the drive-through (see Rule 13 again if you're still unclear on why that's problematic). Almost all of the breakfast options in this book can be made ahead and/or made quickly. I'll accept no excuses for why you can't fit a healthy, real-food breakfast into your routine. Don't forget to wash it all down with a glass or two of water!

RULE 15: MAKE YOUR OWN FOOD AND EAT AT LEAST TEN MEALS A WEEK AT HOME

When you stop eating fast food, you have to start making more of your own meals at home. Go the other way and you still benefit—start making more of your meals at home as a strategy for eliminating fast food!

The basic reason that it's so important to cook for yourself at least once a day (which is what ten times a week amounts to, plus a few days when you have to eat more at home) is that it'll commit you to shopping and planning ahead, which, in turn, means you'll eat better and—if you confront your portion sizes—less. Better doesn't have to mean more time-consuming—most of the recipes in this book are quick and easy—it just means better quality. Need I repeat that better-quality food and less of it leads to weight loss?

In the "Do-Ahead Details" section I'll outline how to stock your fridge and your pantry to set yourself up for success with this rule. Of course, every recipe in this book supports it as well.

RULE 16: BANISH HIGH-SALT FOODS

We humans need salt to stay chemically balanced, but no one needs as much as the average American gets every day (3,400 milligrams), and each person's needs fluctuates—if you work out a lot, you need to get more salt in your diet to replace what you sweat off. If you're a basic couch potato, you're probably getting too much salt in those potato chips next to you! What I want you to do is get down to 2,000 milligrams or less.

Paying attention to food labels (Rule 8) is the best and most effective place to start in this endeavor. From applesauce to tomato soup to peanut butter to canned vegetables, salt happens to be the most common added ingredient in all processed foods. Be careful about what brands you buy, but also beware of processed foods that claim to be "low sodium" or "heart healthy"—that may be the case only if you eat the ridiculously small portion they call a serving!

Another easy and simple way to cut down on your salt? Don't put a salt shaker on the table at home or move it off the table when eating out. So often, we put salt on our food before even tasting it (big mistake). If you put that shaker out of reach, you'll likely notice that most food tastes good—even great—without the added shake.

RULE 17: EAT YOUR VEGETABLES—
JUST DO IT!

Oh, come on—no moaning and complaining! I'm not talking about the boring or mushy vegetables you might have been forced to eat growing up or the kind that your school cafeteria boiled within an inch of their lives.

At almost every grocery store there is now such a beautiful and colorful array of vegetable options (and at most stores, the produce section is right there at the door so you can't miss it) that there is really no excuse for you not to find a way to add them to almost every one of your meals. Vegetables are fashionable now, people. Get with the program!

Of course, this isn't about staying current and fashionable, and you know it. To get to thin, you'll sometimes have to trick yourself into eating fewer calories (as well as less fat), and vegetables can help you do that. You can eat a whole head of broccoli or a whole bag of spinach or a whole package of mushrooms and do no harm. Same goes for the "as much as you want, anytime" list of vegetables in the box on the next page. For starchy or sugary veggies like beets, butternut squash, carrots, pumpkin, yams, and turnips, limit yourself to no more than $1/2$ cup (and not with dinner).

That means you can eat rather enormous volumes of food (vegetables) and never get fat. If you're a person who feels she needs volume and/or has gained weight because you can't stop eating and grazing throughout the day, vegetables are going to turn the tide for you. Eat and graze on them all day and you'll fill up, get tons of fiber (which keeps things moving, if you know what I mean), and meet your oral fixation to be chewing on something all the time.

Please do yourself a favor and commit to eating your vegetables. Stretch outside of your comfort zone and try new ones as often as you can. You'll be surprised by the range of flavors, textures, and colors you will come to love.

AS MUCH AS YOU WANT, ANYTIME VEGGIES:

Artichokes	Garden cress
Arugula	Green beans
Asparagus	Jicama
Bell peppers	Kale
Bok choy	Kohlrabi
Broccoli	Komatsuna (Japanese mustard spinach)
Broccoli rabe	Leeks
Broccoli Romanesco	Lettuces
Broccolini	Mizuna
Brussels sprouts	Mushrooms
Cabbage	Mustard greens
Cauliflower	Onions
Chard	Radishes
Chinese cabbage	Spinach
Collard greens	Tomatoes
Cucumbers	Watercress
Daikon	Yellow summer squash
Eggplant	Zucchini
Fennel	

RULE 18: GO TO BED HUNGRY

How fantastic would it be to burn fat like crazy without having to work out? Pretty fantastic, right? Well, that's what'll happen if you go to bed a little hungry, because when your body is denied fuel for more than five hours, it starts burning fat and sugar. For real. Whether you decide not to eat anything three hours before going to bed or not to eat after a certain time in the evening, you're going to burn fat while you sleep. If you decide to eat nothing after 8 P.M., for instance, you'll start burning fat and sugar by 1 A.M. and you'll keep on burning until you wake up and, literally, break your fast (breakfast).

If you've eaten "lean and green" for dinner like you're supposed to (see Rule 7), you'll be that much better set for the night. An absence of carbs in your bloodstream at bedtime will let your body produce the hormones it needs for better sleep, and with better sleep comes a host of other benefits (see the next rule).

Don't extrapolate from this rule and decide to deny your body fuel for five hours during your waking hours. When you're sleeping you won't notice that you're hungry, and you can eat when you wake up (that real breakfast you've committed to). If you try to fast during the day, you will inevitably become hungry enough to overeat at your next meal (binge!).

RULE 19: SLEEP RIGHT

I need you to hear this and internalize the truth of it: good sleep, which I define as uninterrupted sleep for as close to eight hours as you can manage—is as important to weight loss as any of the other "ingredients" I've listed above. You need to think of it as an important component of your thin lifestyle. You can't get or stay thin long without it.

You probably know that without proper rest your muscles won't have a chance to heal (and what's the point of lifting weights or sweating it out in the gym if you don't give your body a chance to recover and grow stronger from that effort?). Maybe you also know that good sleep gives your brain the time it needs to sort what you learned and saw and experienced during the day.

You're also no doubt aware of what happens when you *don't* get enough sleep: you are less able to think clearly and function at the top of your game the next day. Probably not a good thing for your career or your general mood!

But here's another thing that happens when you don't get enough sleep—you tend to reach for high-calorie foods the next day. Your instinct is perhaps to comfort your sleepy self or to give yourself a little more energy with a sugary treat. But you know what happens after that initial sugar rush, right? You crash—even more tired and less able to think straight than before. Why put yourself in that position? Make getting enough sleep a priority as often as you can. *Plan* those eight hours into your schedule and protect them.

No matter how many of my Skinny Meals you try, and no matter how dedicated you are to the Skinny Rules lifestyle over the long haul, there will come many a day when you are not able to control every meal you eat. You will be invited to someone's house for dinner, to an office party, to a holiday celebration with family; you will have to eat breakfast with colleagues, lunch on the fly, or dinner from take-out containers. These things happen. They are part of life and that's really as it should be; you shouldn't have to sit anything out!

The good news is that my Skinny Rules can accommodate both planned diet interruptions and spontaneous changes of plan. Yes, you get one "splurge" meal a week. Not only do I think everyone should indulge once a week, but psychologically this is an incredibly important rule because it absolves you of the guilt normally associated with "cheating" on a diet. No more beating yourself up for falling off the diet wagon . . . and no more throwing your hands in the air in disgust and deciding that, well, you just can't do this diet after all, so you're giving up on it altogether. No more of that. You get a splurge because I said so.

That said, let's go over just a few splurge rules so that you can enjoy the meal guilt-free:

- Notice I am not saying one splurge *day*—this is a one-meal occasion.
- This splurge meal is yours to pick—breakfast, lunch, or dinner—but when you can arrange or control the invitations, aim for a breakfast or lunch splurge so that you can still abide by Rule 18 (go to bed hungry).
- Don't blow off Rule 1 just because you're splurging—drink water before the meal, drink water with the meal.
- If your splurge meal includes ordering or being served alcohol, stick with red wine and stick with just one glass.
- The only place you can't spend your splurge is a fast-food joint. Eat real food—this is a meal meant to pamper you, and there is nothing about the fast-food experience that pampers you.
- Last but not least: don't splurge alone. Again, this is a meal to savor. Share that with someone special!

DO-AHEAD DETAILS:
SET YOURSELF UP FOR SUCCESS
BY SHOPPING WITH PURPOSE

If your diet has been full of processed foods or grains or you're often guilty of eating out at all the wrong places, you may now feel a tad daunted at the idea of adopting all twenty of my Skinny Rules right away. Some people decide to try to adopt a couple of rules per week and ease themselves into this new Skinny Rules way of life. If that describes you, fine. If you'd rather leap in with both feet, that's even better; you'll see results more quickly. Either way, the following "do-ahead details" will set you up for success and ensure that you have the ingredients on hand to make good food at home and help with your good decision making.

CLEAN OUT YOUR KITCHEN

Get a big garbage bag and prepare to give your kitchen and your life a clean sweep! If any of the following boxes, bags, bottles, or cans are unopened, you can also donate them to a local food pantry. Just keep the following out of yours:

- White flour or non-whole-grain products: bread, tortillas, rice and rice mixes, breakfast bars, pasta, cake, pancake or waffle mixes
- Sugar products: white, confectioners', and brown sugars; artificial

sweeteners and sugar substitutes; ice cream and frozen desserts; boxes of chocolates or candy (get rid of those leftover Halloween treats, people!); jellies and jams; sweet pickles

- White potatoes (including any potato products, like mashed potato flakes, frozen French fries, or hash browns)
- Un-Skinny snacks: potato chips, pretzels, crackers, popcorn, and granola bars
- Store-bought salad dressing, mayonnaise, and canned soups (if your chicken or vegetable broth is not low-sodium, donate it).

RESTOCK YOUR PANTRY

Now that you've banished the things that have been hijacking your health for too long, it's time to replenish your pantry so that you have only the ingredients that will support your weight-loss goals. Make sure you have the following staples.

This restocking shopping list is reprinted at the back of the book so that you can cut it out and bring it with you to the store. With this master list in hand, you can get everything in one trip, thus limiting your "exposure" to the temptations down every grocery aisle!

Drinks

Herbal tea; green tea is best
Coffee or espresso
Seltzer water
Protein powder (egg protein powder or whey protein isolate)

Cooking Oils, Vinegars, Condiments, and Pickled Things

Olive oil (and an olive oil mister so that you can control the amount you use in cooking)
Toasted sesame oil
Coconut oil

Bragg Liquid Aminos

Agave syrup

Good-quality balsamic vinegar—red or white, or both

Red wine vinegar

Apple cider vinegar

Worcestershire sauce

Tabasco sauce

Sriracha hot sauce

Capers

Black olives (canned or fresh, pitted)

Green olives (canned or fresh, pitted)

Small cans of chipotle chiles in adobo sauce

Dijon mustard

Baking Aisle Ingredients

New containers of your favorite dried herbs (see the sidebar on page 25 for the ones I
consider staples)

Vanilla extract

Baking powder

Baking soda

Rolled oats

Ground flaxseed (be sure to store this in your fridge)

Dairy and Cheese

Unsweetened almond milk

Block of parmesan cheese

Canned Goods

Cans or packets of water-packed tuna

Low-sodium canned beans—

     white (cannellini), black, garbanzo, and kidney beans

Low-sodium chicken and vegetable broth

Low-sodium canned crushed tomatoes

Tomato paste

Nuts and Seeds

Pre-portioned packets of raw or dry-roasted almonds

Almond butter or all-natural peanut butter (no sugar added)

Walnuts

Cashews (unsalted, raw)

Pine nuts

Unsalted pepitas (green pumpkin seeds)

Grains and Pasta

Whole-grain pasta or gluten-free pasta—pick any shape you like

Quinoa

Farro

Lentils

Brown rice (individual precooked packages are the best for portion control)

Aromatics

Yellow onions

Red onions

Shallots
Several bulbs of garlic
Ginger root

RESTOCK YOUR REFRIGERATOR (WEEKLY)

At the beginning of each weekly menu, starting on page 171, I give you a list of the refrigerated or fresh staples you will need to shop for that week. If you decide you want to branch out on your own and plan your own Skinny Meals menus, by all means go ahead and make your own lists. But do try to shop for your ingredients (and to replenish any pantry items you're running low on) only once a week. Not only is this an obvious time- and sanity-saving recommendation, but I find it's a good idea to stay out of the grocery store as much as you can, especially when you are trying to get to your goal weight. If you can avoid it, why tempt yourself with those aisles of "easy," "instant," or "meal-starter" options? Get into the habit of shopping with purpose—knowing what you need and not getting more—and make sure that the following ingredients find their way into your carriage regularly:

A dozen eggs (those with added omega-3s are best)

Lean ground turkey

Boneless, skinless chicken breasts

Fish fillets (wrap separately and store in the freezer if you're not going to eat
 within two days)

Tempeh

Low-sodium sliced turkey breast

6-ounce containers of plain nonfat Greek yogurt

Small containers of low-fat cottage cheese

Avocados

Apples

Berries—fresh or frozen (with no added fruit juice or sugars)

Cucumbers (Persian)

Lemons, limes, and oranges (for use in many recipes and to flavor your water)

Sweet potatoes

Mixed salad greens

Spinach and kale and any vegetables you want to try—either in your main meals or for snack time (see page 17 for my list of "As Much as You Want, Anytime Veggies")

Tomatoes

Fresh herbs (parsley, basil, and cilantro show up in many of my recipes)

Frozen Foods

Ezekiel bread and tortillas

Frozen berries (no sugar or fruit juice added)

Frozen peas

PART II

SKINNY MEALS

Avocado Toast

Replace the fatty butter and sugary jam you used to pile on your toast with this abundance of natural flavors, good fats, and protein and you will have a well-balanced meal to kick-start your day! It's low calorie, high protein, and oh so good!

1/4 avocado

Pinch of paprika

1/2 teaspoon freshly squeezed lemon juice

1 slice whole-wheat or Ezekiel bread, toasted

4 hard-boiled large egg whites, chopped

1 1/2 teaspoons finely diced shallots

1 teaspoon Dijon mustard

1/2 teaspoon capers, rinsed and coarsely chopped

Dash of freshly ground black pepper

In a small bowl, mash and mix the avocado, paprika, and lemon juice. Spread on the toast.

In the same small bowl, mix together the egg whites, shallots, mustard, capers, and pepper.

Pile the egg white mixture on top of the avocado-smeared toast and enjoy!

Nutrition information: 221 calories, 20g protein, 20g carbs, 8g fat, 6g fiber

Like most busy people, I tend to automate my weekday breakfasts—I have one or two recipes that I repeat, saving the slightly more complicated preparations for weekends, when I have more time to cook. Avocado toast is one I just have to have several times a week! To save even more time in the morning, double the chopped egg white, caper, shallot, and Dijon mixture the first day of the week you make this breakfast—it'll keep in your refrigerator and then all you have to do is pile it on your toast with the mashed avocado.

Apple Pie Shake

Have your pie and drink it, too! With this breakfast, you can enjoy the flavors of a classic dessert in a way that still meets my approval—you'll experience the comfort of apple pie without the outrageous calories. The almond butter gives you hunger-satisfying protein, and with just the right amount of carbs and fat, you'll get a jump on the day without hurting your waistline.

 Meatless day option!

¹/₂ small banana, frozen

¹/₂ apple, sliced

1 scoop of vanilla protein powder

Pinch of cinnamon

Pinch of nutmeg

¹/₂ cup crushed ice

1 tablespoon almond butter

Combine all of the ingredients in a blender and blend until smooth.

Nutrition information: 271 calories, 18g protein, 32g carbs, 10g fat, 8g fiber

Using a frozen banana thickens up this drink, making it seem both more ice creamy and sinful (yum) and requiring you to slow down when drinking it (to avoid getting an instant "frozen brain" headache!). If you forget to put a banana in the freezer the night before, however, you can certainly use a room-temperature banana—just add some more ice and you'll get a similar effect.

Spicy Green Shake

The heat from the peppers and spices in this recipe will boost your metabolism (and your morning) into high gear, and the added spinach and kale will give you the iron and energy of Popeye. Since you're blending this, leave on the kiwi skin—it has a ton of fiber, and you know you need your fiber!

1 kiwi, unpeeled and cut into quarters

1 Persian cucumber, diced

1 cup chopped fresh spinach

1 cup chopped kale

1 tablespoon freshly squeezed lemon juice

1/8 teaspoon cayenne pepper

1/2 pear, unpeeled and diced

2 tablespoons ground flaxseed

Combine all of the ingredients in a blender and blend until smooth.

Serve with a side of My Skinny Scramble (see box).

Nutrition information: 306 calories, 25g protein, 33g carbs, 10g fat, 12g fiber

---

MY SKINNY SCRAMBLE

When you're eating the Skinny Rules way, I want women to get 1,200 calories a day, so you're going to prepare My Skinny Scramble using a 3+1 ratio (3 egg whites plus 1 whole egg). Men, you can go with the 5+1 ratio (5 egg whites plus 1 whole egg), because you need 1,500 calories a day. Either way, it's protein power you're getting in this quick-prep side. Simply beat the whites and the one egg together and quickly scramble in a nonstick frying pan (or add just a spritz of olive oil or canola oil spray to a standard pan). Any recipe that calls for the addition of My Skinny Scramble (or that calls for a 3+1 or 5+1 egg ratio as part of the ingredients list) gives you the nutritional information for the 3+1 ratio. Just so you know, here is the full info on both ratios.

Nutrition Information: 5+1 = 146 calories, 25g protein, 0g carbs, 4.4g fat

3+1 = 112 calories, 17.5g protein, 0g carbs, 4.4g fat

Peachy Keen Smoothie

You can use another fresh summer stone fruit like a nectarine, plum, or apricot for this recipe. During the winter or other times when you don't have access to fresh fruit, use frozen fruit (but make sure no sugar was added!). Add a 3+1 or 5+1 Skinny Scramble on the side (see page 33) and you won't be hungry for hours!

Meatless day option!

1/2 peach, coarsely chopped

1/3 cup frozen mixed berries

1/3 cup plain nonfat Greek yogurt

1 Persian cucumber, diced

2 tablespoons ground flaxseed

Combine all of the ingredients in a blender and blend until smooth.

Serve with a side of My Skinny Scramble (page 33).

Nutrition information: 291 calories, 28g protein, 29g carbs, 10g fat, 7g fiber

You can buy flaxseed whole or ground (flax meal) in most supermarkets these days. You'll want to use flax meal here because your body can better absorb the healthful properties when the seeds are broken down from the start. Whether you buy the whole seeds and grind them yourself (use a coffee grinder and it's done in seconds) or buy the preground meal, remember to store the flax in the fridge, where it will keep longer.

Leaner Loco Moco

There's a dish in Hawaii called "Loco Moco." It's rice topped with beef patties, gravy, and fried eggs. Not exactly a Skinny Meal, but it inspired this recipe! I use brown rice here, and the mushrooms create a "meaty" topping with the eggs.

Olive oil spray

4 crimini or button mushrooms, quartered

2 cups coarsely chopped fresh spinach

1 teaspoon Bragg Liquid Aminos

$1/2$ to 1 teaspoon Sriracha, to taste

3+1 or 5+1 large eggs, beaten (see page 33)

$1/2$ cup cooked brown rice, warmed

Spray a medium skillet with olive oil and heat over medium-high heat.

Add the mushrooms and cook for 3 minutes without stirring. Stir once and cook for 3 more minutes, again undisturbed.

Add the spinach and wilt. Stir in the Bragg Aminos and Sriracha, then pour in the eggs.

Cook, stirring occasionally, until the eggs are scrambled. Serve over the brown rice.

Nutrition information: 260 calories, 22g protein, 28g carbs, 7g fat, 5g fiber

Since Skinny Rule 7 dictates no carbs after the midday meal, help yourself to brown rice in the morning with this recipe. Many grocery chains now sell single-serving packages of rice that can be microwaved in just a few minutes, but if you can't find that product, cook up a couple of servings of rice on the weekend—then all you'll have to do is heat it up.

Overloaded Toast

Just because I tell you not to butter your toast doesn't mean you need to eat it dry. The natural sugars in berries—blueberries, raspberries, blackberries, strawberries, or a combination—give you the sweetness you might be craving, not to mention a treat for the eyes as well. Unsweetened almond butter is a healthy fat and will be the delicious glue that holds your berries in place.

The powerful protein an egg white scramble provides is an invaluable way to fill up in the morning ... keeping you satisfied for longer over the course of the day. If you're pressed for time, you certainly don't have to add these to your morning menu, but don't you *want* to eat more if you can? Of course you do!

1 tablespoon unsweetened almond butter

1 slice of Ezekiel bread, toasted

$1/2$ cup berries

4 large egg whites, scrambled

Spread the almond butter on your toast and press as many berries as will fit on top.

Serve with a side of scrambled egg whites.

Nutrition information: 276 calories, 21g protein, 29g carbs, 9g fat, 9g fiber

Greek Yogurt Waffles

My Skinny Meals replace unhealthy ingredients with ones that can benefit you. In this case, the Greek yogurt replaces the fat that normally comes from added butter, buttermilk, or cream. And coconut oil (which is a healthy fat, though it surely doesn't *look* healthier since it comes as a solid that looks a lot like lard) replaces traditional baking oils like canola or vegetable oil.

2 cups rolled oats

½ teaspoon salt

1 teaspoon baking soda

½ teaspoon cinnamon

1 tablespoon agave

¾ cup unsweetened almond milk (plus a little more to thin, if necessary)

¼ cup plain nonfat Greek yogurt

1 large egg

⅛ cup coconut oil, melted

½ teaspoon vanilla extract

Heat a waffle iron.

In a blender, add oats and grind until they reach a flour consistency.

Add salt, baking soda, and cinnamon and pulse 2 to 3 times to combine.

Add the wet ingredients and puree until smooth.

Lightly grease the waffle iron with cooking spray and pour in ⅓ cup of the batter.

Cook the waffle for 4 to 5 minutes, or until the waffle iron alerts that it's ready. Repeat with the remaining batter.

Makes 5 waffles (5 servings)

Nutrition information per serving: 204 calories, 7g protein, 26g carbs, 9g fat, 3g fiber

Waffles don't have to weigh you down and they don't have to be slathered with butter and syrup to taste great. Because of the agave and coconut oil, these waffles will add a surprisingly sweet note to your morning. Add a handful of mixed berries on top for color, taste, and your daily berry fix (Rule 6). Refrigerate the extra waffles (this recipe makes five, which equals five servings) in an airtight container and toast them up each morning you want to feel like you're indulging in a restaurant brunch!

Baked Quinoatmeal

Quinoa is a high-fiber, protein-packed superfood. Get used to saying it (keen-wah) and putting it into your menu rotation! It's a carbohydrate, but remember that Rule 7 allows you carbs for breakfast (and lunch), so go for it and feel full all morning.

 Meatless day option!

4 large egg whites

1 teaspoon olive oil

1/4 cup unsweetened vanilla almond milk

1 teaspoon agave

1/2 cup cooked quinoa

1/4 cup raspberries

1/4 cup strawberries, quartered

Olive oil spray

Don't discount this one just because you're on the run. If you whisk the ingredients together and pop the concoction in the oven before you shower, it'll be done—hot and irresistible—by the time you're dressed and ready to go! Of course, it can also be made ahead of time and stored in the fridge for an easy microwavable takeaway on rushed mornings.

Preheat the oven to 375°F.

Beat the egg whites, olive oil, almond milk, and agave.

Fold in the quinoa and berries.

Lightly coat a ramekin or small baking dish with olive oil spray. Pour in the quinoa-berry mixture.

Bake for 15 to 20 minutes, until the liquids have been absorbed.

Nutrition information: 327 calories, 21g protein, 44g carbs, 8g fat, 6g fiber

Quinoa Cakes

Eat these quinoa cakes hot out of the oven or make them ahead and store in the fridge overnight. If spinach and broccoli aren't your thing, you can substitute almost any vegetable—try chopped bell peppers, cauliflower, or kale.

3 large egg whites plus 1 whole egg

1 tablespoon chopped fresh parsley

Pinch of freshly ground black pepper

1/2 cup cooked quinoa

1 cup chopped fresh spinach

1 cup coarsely chopped broccoli

Olive oil spray

Preheat the oven to 350°F.

Beat the eggs with the parsley and pepper.

Fold in the quinoa, spinach, and broccoli.

Lightly coat 3 muffin cups with olive oil spray and spoon a third of the mixture into each.

Bake for 20 to 25 minutes, until the liquid has been absorbed and the cakes are firm.

This recipe helps you live up to Skinny Rule 17—Eat Your Veggies! Come to think of it, it adheres to several rules—Rule 16 about sodium, Rule 7 about carbs in the morning, and Rule 4 about cutting back on processed grains. But really, the prize ingredients here are the veggies. As you know, I try to sneak veggies into every meal possible—you will never get fat eating vegetables, but they will help you fill up. That's a good thing!

Nutrition information: 316 calories, 27g protein, 36g carbs, 8g fat, 6g fiber

Eggs Florentine

Will you take a look at that photo!? Doesn't it look like something you could serve for a brunch with pride and confidence? Well, go ahead! But don't forget to make this just for yourself sometimes, too.

SAUCE:

1/4 cup plain 2% fat Greek yogurt

1 teaspoon Dijon mustard

1/2 teaspoon chopped fresh dill

1/2 teaspoon chopped fresh parsley

EGGS:

2 cups coarsely chopped fresh spinach

1 whole-wheat English muffin, toasted

3+1 or 5+1 large eggs, scrambled (see page 33)

Instead of making a traditional Hollandaise sauce (a sinfully rich combination of egg yolks and melted butter that hurts my heart just thinking about it), I've lightened things up using Greek yogurt. I don't think you're going to miss "real" Hollandaise—this is going to become your go-to sauce for life.

Mix the sauce ingredients together and set aside so that it has a chance to come to room temperature while you are preparing the spinach and eggs.

In a steamer, steam the spinach for 30 seconds to 1 minute, or until just wilted. Drain any excess water. Set aside.

Top the toasted English muffin with the spinach and eggs; delicately spoon the sauce on top.

Nutrition information: 313 calories, 30g protein, 32g carbs, 8g fat, 6g fiber

Skinny Latkes

Remember Rule 11? No more white potatoes. Here we'll use nutritionally rich sweet potatoes instead. And adding the egg and asparagus takes your morning to a whole new nutritional level!

LATKES:

1/2 cup shredded raw sweet potato

1 large egg white

1 tablespoon ground flaxseed

1/2 garlic clove, crushed

Olive oil spray

SAUCE:

1/4 cup plain 2% fat Greek yogurt

1 teaspoon Dijon mustard

1/2 teaspoon chopped fresh dill

1 large egg + 1 egg white (for women) or
    2 large eggs +1 egg white (for men), beaten

6 asparagus spears, steamed

Though pan-frying a potato pancake might remind you of your grandmother's process, you'll be sautéing (with just a spritz of oil) from now on. You could also bake them (at 350°F for 12 to 15 minutes, flipping halfway through). I think Grandma would still approve—these latkes are delicious and have a satisfying "chew" to them, too!

Mix the sweet potato, egg white, flaxseed, and garlic in a bowl.

Using your hands, form into 2 potato pancakes.

Coat a medium skillet with olive oil spray and place over medium-high heat. When a drop of water sizzles in the hot pan, add both pancakes and cook for 5 minutes on each side.

In the meantime, mix the sauce ingredients in a bowl. Scramble the eggs in a frying pan.

When the pancakes are done, top with the eggs, then the asparagus, and, finally, a delicate dollop of the sauce.

Nutrition information: 296 calories, 25g protein, 30g carbs, 9g fat, 7g fiber

Breakfast Tacos

Want an extra metabolism boost this morning? Drizzle your favorite hot sauce on your breakfast taco. To turn this recipe into something more like huevos rancheros, simmer the pico de gallo ingredients to warm them up, then crisp up your tortillas by quickly toasting them one at a time over the flame of your gas stove, holding them in tongs and fanning them across the flames for about 15 seconds (don't place them on the flames or grill itself—you'll either burn the tortillas or start a fire!). If you have an electric stove, toast the tortillas in a hot skillet coated with olive oil spray.

Olive oil spray

2 4^1/$_2$-inch whole-wheat tortillas

2 cups chopped fresh spinach

3+1 or 5+1 large eggs, beaten (see page 33)

1 cup Pico de Gallo (see sidebar)

Lightly coat a medium skillet with olive oil spray. Heat the tortillas over medium-high heat, turning once, and set aside.

Coat the skillet with olive oil spray again and add the spinach. Cook until wilted, just a minute or two, then add the eggs and scramble.

Top the tortillas with the eggs and my Pico de Gallo.

MY PICO DE GALLO

Here's my quick recipe for pico de gallo. This recipe makes about two cups.

4 plum tomatoes, chopped

^{1}/$_4$ cup finely chopped red onion

1 to 2 tablespoons finely chopped fresh cilantro, to taste

1 small jalapeño pepper, seeded and chopped

1 small garlic clove, crushed

1^1/$_2$ teaspoons freshly squeezed lime juice

Lightly toss all of the ingredients and store in an airtight container in the fridge.

Nutritional info per serving: 39 calories, 2g protein, 9g carbs, 0g fat, 2g fiber

---

Nutrition information: 254 calories, 23g protein, 25g carbs, 7g fat, 6g fiber

Overloaded Baked Potato

Skinny Rule 17 encourages you to fill up with vegetables any and every time you can. Here's an opportunity to load up and keep yourself full for a long time. If you want more than a cup of veggies with your sweet potato, knock yourself out! A dollop of Greek yogurt nicely mimics sour cream.

1 medium sweet potato (unpeeled)
Olive oil spray
1 cup chopped veggies (spinach, zucchini, broccoli, peppers, tomato)
3+1 or 5+1 large eggs, beaten (see page 33)
2 tablespoons plain 2% fat Greek yogurt

Puncture the sweet potato with a fork four or five times. Place on a microwavable dish and microwave on high power for 5 to 8 minutes, until soft. (Start checking after 5 minutes; microwaves vary.)

Meanwhile, coat a medium skillet with olive oil spray and sauté the veggies over medium heat until cooked through, about 5 minutes.

Add the eggs to the veggies and scramble.

Carefully take the sweet potato out of the microwave (it will be very hot) and cut lengthwise.

Top the sweet potato with the veggie/egg scramble and top with a dollop of Greek yogurt.

Nutrition information: 246 calories, 65g protein, 22g carbs, 7g fat, 6g fiber

Wild Mushroom Omelet

Mushrooms are loaded with nutrients (vitamin B$_6$) and fiber (Skinny Rule 5!) and they add a depth of flavor to anything you add them to. Remember, though, that they hold a lot of water and will make your omelet runny and loose if you don't cook them down first to extract their liquid.

1 cup mixed mushrooms (crimini, shiitake, porcini, portobello)

1 teaspoon olive oil

1 tablespoon chopped shallots

1/2 teaspoon chopped garlic

2 tablespoons chopped fresh parsley

Olive oil spray

3+1 or 5+1 large eggs, beaten (see page 33)

1 slice whole-wheat or Ezekiel bread, toasted

> Never wash mushrooms under water! They'll absorb the rinsing water and you'll be left with waterlogged blobs. Instead, just lightly brush the dirt away with a damp paper towel.

Remove the stems from the mushrooms. Clean the mushroom caps by wiping with a damp paper towel, then cut into equal slices.

Heat the olive oil in a medium skillet; add the shallots and cook over low heat for 5 minutes.

Add the mushrooms and cook over medium heat for 5 minutes, stirring only every minute or so.

Stir in the garlic and cook for 2 more minutes.

Toss in the parsley, then transfer the mixture to a bowl and set aside.

Wipe the pan with a paper towel, then coat with olive oil spray and set over low heat. Pour in the eggs, making sure they spread evenly throughout the pan. After about 20 seconds, roll the pan around so the liquid eggs fill the empty spots. When the eggs are cooked through and no longer runny, cover one half with the mushrooms, then fold the other half over to make an omelet.

Gently slide the omelet onto a plate. Serve with toast.

Nutrition information: 265 calories, 24g protein, 20g carbs, 10g fat, 4g fiber

Red Egg Skillet

Eggs are a perfect canvas for herb and spice experimentation. A common Mexican flavor combination is cumin and oregano. Add a little paprika, cayenne, and parsley and you're approximating a common Portuguese combination. Play with your flavor combinations to make your morning meal just right for you—even with all that extra seasoning, you aren't adding any dreaded sodium.

1/2 teaspoon olive oil

1 cup chopped red bell peppers

1/2 garlic clove, crushed

1/3 cup low-sodium crushed tomatoes

Pinch of paprika

Pinch of ground cumin

Pinch of cayenne pepper

Pinch of dried oregano

3+1 or 5+1 large eggs (see page 33)

1 cup chopped fresh spinach

1 tablespoon chopped fresh parsley

1 slice whole-wheat or Ezekiel bread, toasted

Preheat the oven to 350°F.

Coat a medium ovenproof nonstick skillet with the olive oil and sauté the bell peppers over medium-high heat until cooked through, about 5 minutes. Add the garlic, tomatoes, paprika, cumin, cayenne, and oregano and simmer for 4 to 5 more minutes.

Beat the eggs with the spinach and pour into the skillet. Lightly stir with a wooden spoon to make sure the eggs are evenly distributed throughout the pan.

Place the skillet in the oven and bake for 15 to 20 minutes or until the eggs are cooked through.

Top with parsley and serve with toast.

Nutrition information: 280 calories, 24g protein, 29g carbs, 10g fat, 6g fiber

Blueberry Muffins

I've heard it said that muffins are just a marketing invention to get us to eat cake for breakfast. That may be true, but my muffins use rolled oats instead of processed white flour, so you can have your "cake" and eat it too! Blueberries aren't the only fruit you can use—let the seasonal produce inspire your choice.

1 teaspoon ground cinnamon

1/2 teaspoon grated lemon zest

2 tablespoons ground flaxseed

8 large egg whites

1 cup rolled oats (not instant)

1/2 cup unsweetened applesauce

1/2 cup fresh blueberries

Preheat the oven to 350°F.

Blend all ingredients except the blueberries in a food processor or blender until smooth. Fold in the blueberries.

Line 4 muffin cups with paper liners.

Fill the lined cups with the mixture and bake for 20 to 30 minutes, until a toothpick inserted in the center of a muffin comes out clean.

Makes 4 muffins (2 servings)

Nutrition information per serving: 294 calories, 21g protein, 42g carbs, 6g fat, 8g fiber

Sweet Potato Baked Eggs

You could scramble the eggs and potato/veggie mix and it would taste just as yummy, but baking it in a ramekin is an elegant presentation and a small gift to yourself at the beginning of the day.

1 teaspoon olive oil

1/2 cup cubed sweet potato

3 asparagus spears, chopped

1 teaspoon chopped fresh rosemary

1/2 teaspoon chopped fresh thyme

Pinch of crushed red pepper

1 cup chopped fresh spinach

Olive oil spray

3+1 or 5+1 large eggs, beaten (see page 33)

> With this dish, you can get really creative. Whether it's the herbs you use or the vegetables you add, don't be afraid to try new combinations. Fresh thyme and rosemary are a power couple, but parsley is also a good option and dried herbs work well, too.

Preheat the oven to 375°F.

Heat a medium skillet over medium heat. Coat with the olive oil. Add the sweet potatoes and cover. Cook for 5 minutes, stirring occasionally.

Add the asparagus, rosemary, thyme, and crushed red pepper. Sauté for another 3 minutes. Add the spinach and stir until wilted. Remove from the heat.

Lightly coat a ramekin or small baking dish with olive oil spray. Pour in the potato and vegetable mixture and add the eggs.

Bake for 15 to 20 minutes, until the eggs are fully cooked.

Nutrition information: 251 calories, 20g protein, 21g carbs, 10g fat, 4g fiber

Mini Lemon Ricotta Pancakes with Fruit Reduction

Combining the bright flavor of lemon with the natural sweetness and color of berries will give you the zing of spring anytime. Frozen berries will work just as well.

REDUCED BERRIES:

1/2 cup mixed berries (or just one variety of berry—whatever you have on hand)

1/2 teaspoon agave

1 tablespoon freshly squeezed lemon juice

1 tablespoon water

PANCAKES:

1/2 teaspoon olive oil

1/3 cup rolled oats (not instant)

1/4 cup skim-milk ricotta

4 large egg whites

1/8 teaspoon baking powder

1/2 teaspoon vanilla extract

1/4 teaspoon grated lemon zest

> The oils in the skin of a lemon pack a punch and will really give these pancakes a distinct and welcome freshness. Remember to wash the outside of the lemon prior to zesting, and make sure you don't grate into the white because the pith is really bitter.

In a small pot, heat the berries with the agave, lemon juice, and water and simmer over low heat for 5 minutes. Remove from the heat and set aside.

Coat a large skillet with the olive oil and heat over medium heat.

In a medium bowl, lightly stir the oats, ricotta, egg whites, baking powder, vanilla, and lemon zest until well combined.

When the skillet is hot (a drop of batter should sizzle immediately), pour 4 separate dollops of batter to form mini pancakes.

Cook for about 90 seconds per side, flipping once.

Top with the reduced berries.

Nutrition information: 318 calories, 25g protein, 34g carbs, 10g fat, 6g fiber

Breakfast Burrito Bowl

No tortilla, no sour cream, no greasy cheese, no fun? Not at all! Try this light and satisfying version of what is typically a heavy, greasy, and guilt-inducing meal. Cereal isn't the only breakfast you can eat from a bowl!

MY GUACAMOLE

1 avocado, cut into chunks

2 tablespoons finely chopped red onion

1 tablespoon chopped fresh cilantro

1 teaspoon freshly squeezed lime juice

1/2 garlic clove, minced

1 tomato, chopped

1 tablespoon chopped jalapeño pepper

Mix all of the ingredients together with a fork, mashing the avocado to your desired smoothness.

Serves 4

3 large egg whites

1 tablespoon plain nonfat Greek yogurt

Olive oil spray

1/4 cup black beans, rinsed and drained

1 tablespoon chopped fresh cilantro

1 plum tomato, chopped

1/2 teaspoon chili powder

1 cup chopped kale

2 tablespoons Guacamole (see sidebar)

1/4 cup Pico de Gallo (page 45)

Beat the egg whites with the yogurt. Spray a small nonstick skillet with olive oil and heat over medium heat. Pour the mixture into the pan and scramble to your liking. Remove the eggs from the pan and set aside.

In a small saucepan, mix the black beans, cilantro, tomato, and chili powder; cook over medium heat for 5 minutes, stirring occasionally.

In the meantime, place the kale in a steamer and steam for 1 to 2 minutes. Drain the excess liquid, then place the kale in a serving bowl.

Top the kale with the black bean mixture, eggs, and a dollop of guacamole and pico de gallo.

Nutrition information: 261 calories, 23g protein, 28g carbs, 8g fat, 10g fiber

Power Wrap

Breakfast should not stress you out. Breakfast should empower you like this one does—powerful protein in a burrito-like package!

Olive oil spray

1 Ezekiel tortilla

3+1 or 5+1 large eggs, beaten (see page 33)

4 slices low-sodium deli turkey, chopped

Lightly coat a medium nonstick skillet with olive oil spray. Heat the tortilla over medium-high heat, turning once, and set aside.

Coat the skillet with olive oil spray again. Over medium heat, scramble the eggs with the turkey. Stuff them into the tortilla and fold it like a burrito.

Nutrition information: 288 calories, 25g protein, 26g carbs, 9g fat, 5g fiber

A lack of time in the morning often leads to unhealthy and unskinny eating. If you can't slow down, you can at least plan ahead. If you've stocked up on turkey and tortillas (see pages 21 to 26 for other pantry and do-ahead ideas), you can have this breakfast prepared in just a few minutes—and stay satisfied for hours.

LEAN LUNCHES

As you know from Rule 7, your carb eating can extend through lunch, which is why you'll find recipes in this section that include bread, quinoa, tortillas, and pasta. As with the breakfasts, however, these recipes aim to get more protein, fiber, and vegetables into your system while at the same time going low on sodium and fat. I've worked hard to balance these meals for you and to factor them into the rest of your eating day, so I want you to make them, make them again, add vegetables wherever you can or want to, and . . . enjoy!

Peach Salad with Chicken

For added depth of flavor, try grilling the fruit. The scorching heat will crystallize the natural sugars in the fruit, bringing out an unexpected yet savory level of flavors. Paired with summer herbs, like basil, and the peppery bite of arugula, this becomes a crisp yet filling salad.

1 ripe peach, cut into 8 wedges

4 or 5 basil leaves, cut into a chiffonade
(stack the leaves, roll into a "cigar,"
and cut into thin ribbons)

1 mint leaf, cut into slivers

1/4 small red onion, very thinly sliced

1 cup arugula

1 cup baby spinach

4 ounces roasted boneless, skinless
chicken breast, shredded

DRESSING:

1 teaspoon olive oil

1 tablespoon freshly squeezed lemon juice

1 1/2 teaspoons white wine vinegar or apple cider vinegar

1 1/2 teaspoons agave

> You can use other summer stone fruits—nectarines, plums, apricots—which tend to be available around the same time as peaches. In the fall or winter, you can use pears or apples (which helps you meet Rule 6).

Toss the salad ingredients. Mix the dressing ingredients, drizzle over the salad, and serve.

Nutrition information: 249 calories, 25g protein, 24g carbs, 8g fat, 4g fiber

Saucy Spring Roll

In Asian cuisines, a spring roll is typically wrapped in rice paper and filled with rice noodles, shrimp, and veggies. Here, I've replaced the rice paper with an Ezekiel tortilla to help you meet your fiber goals (Rule 5!).

To make this a meatless meal, replace the shrimp with tempeh.

SAUCE:

1 teaspoon unsweetened almond butter

1 teaspoon rice wine vinegar

1 teaspoon Bragg Liquid Aminos

$1/2$ teaspoon agave

$1/4$ teaspoon toasted sesame oil

SPRING ROLL:

3 ounces cooked shrimp (or $1/4$ cup steamed tempeh)

$1/4$ cup shredded carrots

$1/2$ cup shredded red cabbage

1 Persian cucumber, thinly sliced

$1 1/2$ teaspoons chopped unsalted peanuts

1 Ezekiel tortilla

> The sauce recipe here is so fabulous you may want to use it as a condiment for other meals as well. It's a light, semisweet version of the peanutty dipping sauce often served alongside spring rolls and chicken skewers in restaurants.

In a medium bowl, mix the sauce ingredients.

Toss the shrimp (or the tempeh, for a meatless meal), carrots, red cabbage, cucumber, and peanuts in the sauce.

Spoon into the tortilla.

Nutrition information: 310 calories, 25g protein, 39g carbs, 10g fat, 5g fiber
Meatless option: 300 calories, 15g protein, 43g carbs, 12g fat, 5g fiber

Perfect Pasta Salad

Pasta is a great holder of flavors but doesn't bring much to the party on its own. Pair your midday carbs with vegetables, drizzle with a light dressing, and cheers to your health!

To make this a meatless meal, replace the chicken with garbanzo, cannellini, or kidney beans.

$1/4$ cup (2 ounces) uncooked whole-grain or gluten-free pasta

4 ounces roasted boneless, skinless chicken breast, cut into cubes
(or $1/3$ cup garbanzo, cannellini, or kidney beans)

2 plum tomatoes, chopped

1 cup coarsely chopped arugula

1 cup coarsely chopped fresh spinach

2 tablespoons chopped fresh basil

1 tablespoon balsamic vinegar

1 teaspoon olive oil

> In store-prepared pasta salad, any added veggies are usually an afterthought. How can that be called salad? It doesn't have to be that way! My version makes veggies the star—as they should be—and puts the pasta there for just a little added texture and bite.

Cook the pasta according to package directions. Drain and rinse under cold water.

In a bowl, mix the remaining ingredients. Toss with the pasta and chill.

Nutrition information: 275 calories, 28g protein, 26g carbs, 9g fat, 6g fiber
Meatless option: 241 calories, 11g protein, 40g carbs, 6g fat, 11g fiber

Pesto Quesadilla

Grilling or sautéing the tortilla in this recipe (instead of microwaving) adds a textural element that will make you forget you're not using much cheese!

To make this a meatless meal, swap the chicken with cannellini or navy beans.

1 to 2 tablespoons Skinny Pesto (see sidebar)

1 Ezekiel or whole-wheat tortilla

4 ounces roasted boneless, skinless chicken breast, shredded (or $1/3$ cup cannellini or navy beans, smashed)

2 cups chopped fresh spinach

1 tablespoon shredded low-fat mozzarella cheese

1 plum tomato, thinly sliced

Olive oil spray

Spread the pesto evenly on the tortilla. Place the chicken (or beans, for a meatless option), spinach, mozzarella, and tomato on half of the tortilla. Fold the other half of the tortilla over the filling.

Lightly coat a skillet with olive oil spray and set over medium-high heat.

Place the quesadilla on the skillet and cook for 3 minutes on each side.

> **MY SKINNY PESTO**
>
> Here's my pesto recipe, first shared in *The Skinny Rules*:
>
> 1 cup chopped fresh basil
>
> 1 tablespoon grated parmesan cheese
>
> 1 garlic clove
>
> $1 1/2$ teaspoons freshly squeezed lemon juice
>
> 2 tablespoons chopped walnuts, cashews, or pine nuts
>
> Blend all of the ingredients in the bowl of a food processor. Store in the refrigerator for up to 5 days, or freeze. Makes four servings.

Nutrition information: 327 calories, 32g protein, 30g carbs, 9g fat, 6g fiber
Meatless option: 270 calories, 14g protein, 42g carbs, 6g fat, 8g fiber

"Makes Me Happy" Egg Salad Sandwich

In *The Skinny Rules* I shared my "Makes Me Happy" Tuna Salad recipe. This egg salad makes me happy too! It's tasty and lean protein at its best.

2 tablespoons plain 2% fat Greek yogurt

1 teaspoon Dijon mustard

1 teaspoon chopped fresh tarragon

1/2 teaspoon snipped fresh chives

4 hard-boiled large egg whites, chopped

2 tablespoons mashed avocado

1 slice of Ezekiel bread, toasted

Handful of mixed salad greens

In a bowl, mix the yogurt, mustard, tarragon, and chives. Stir in the egg whites until well combined.

Spread the avocado on the toast; top with the greens and the egg white salad.

Nutrition information: 277 calories, 26g protein, 25g carbs, 9g fat, 7g fiber

Ditching the egg yolk helps you ditch calories as well and leaves you with the blank canvas of the lean-protein whites. Tarragon is a great herb to reach for—it adds a clean and unexpected flavor to everything it touches. Thyme would be very nice as well.

Hummus Roll-Up with Roasted Veggies and Turkey

Hummus is versatile and can be flavored in many different ways by using almost any herb or spice. Use my hummus as a condiment in sandwiches or wraps that call for any kind of mayo or aioli.

1 tablespoon My Signature No-Oil Hummus (see sidebar)

2 tablespoons mashed avocado

1 Ezekiel or whole-wheat tortilla

4 ounces sliced low-sodium deli turkey

1/2 cup chopped roasted veggies

Spread the hummus and avocado evenly on the tortilla, then layer with turkey and roasted veggies. Roll like a burrito and enjoy.

Nutrition information: 240 calories, 19g protein, 28g carbs, 7g fat, 5g fiber

MY SIGNATURE NO-OIL HUMMUS

My hummus recipe is also in *The Skinny Rules*. Notice that I use broth instead of tahini and olive oil to do the job of adding flavor and cutting calories and fat.

2 tablespoons freshly squeezed lemon juice

1/4 teaspoon salt

1 15.5-ounce can low-sodium garbanzo beans, drained and rinsed

1/2 garlic clove, cut into a few smaller pieces

1/4 cup low-sodium vegetable broth (or water) to thin

Place all of the ingredients in the bowl of a food processor; process until smooth. Refrigerate in an airtight container for up to 5 days.

Veggie Carbonara

Remember that you can have pasta at lunch when eating the Skinny Rules way. This is a low-calorie and low-fat twist on carbonara that tastes as sinful as the full-fat dish—why would you expect anything less?!

1/2 teaspoon olive oil

1/2 large zucchini, sliced into thin rounds

1/2 garlic clove, crushed

1/3 cup halved cherry tomatoes

Pinch of crushed red pepper

1/3 cup low-sodium vegetable broth

1/2 cup cooked whole-grain or gluten-free spaghetti

3 large egg whites plus 1 whole egg

1 tablespoon chopped fresh basil

Heat the olive oil in a large skillet over medium heat. Add the zucchini, garlic, tomatoes, crushed red pepper, and broth. Stir and cover. Reduce the heat to low and simmer for 5 to 6 minutes, stirring occasionally.

Add the cooked pasta and fold it into the sauce. Cover and cook for about 2 minutes, until heated through.

Beat the eggs in a small bowl. Slowly pour the eggs into the pasta while stirring. Continue to stir until the eggs are cooked through.

Serve, garnished with fresh basil.

Nutrition information: 299 calories, 23g protein, 35g carbs, 9g fat, 6g fiber

A traditional carbonara sauce combines bacon (or pancetta), black pepper, and a creamy egg finish. Clearly, not a Skinny Meal! But the combination of egg whites (and one full egg) and garlic, basil, and veggies is just as satisfying and is yet another way to make sure you are adhering to Rule 17.

Terrific Tuna Salad

Pairing the protein of tuna with the carbs of pasta and all these delicious briny add-ins makes a memorable and hearty lunchtime meal.

4 ounces canned tuna, drained

1 teaspoon capers, rinsed

1/2 shallot, minced

1 tablespoon pitted kalamata olives

1/2 cup cooked whole-wheat corkscrew pasta

1/4 cup quartered cherry tomatoes

1 cup chopped arugula

1 cup chopped fresh spinach

When shopping for canned ingredients, like tuna, be sure to purchase the low-sodium version. There's no short supply of other salty flavors in this dish—capers and olives both naturally add a little salty punch to every bite. For a little extra crunch, you could also dice up a tart apple and mix it into this lunch—and satisfy Rule 6 at the same time!

In a medium bowl, mix the tuna, capers, shallot, and olives.

Toss the pasta, tomatoes, arugula, and spinach with the tuna mixture.

Nutrition information: 288 calories, 28g protein, 26g carbs, 10g fat, 5g fiber

New Mexican Quinoa Salad

A signature feature of Southwestern cuisine, New Mexican green chiles are an amazing ingredient. But if you can't get them where you are, a plain old green bell pepper will do.

1 New Mexican chili or 1 green bell pepper

1 cup steamed kale

2 ounces roasted boneless, skinless chicken breast, cut into cubes

$1/3$ cup halved cherry tomatoes

$1/3$ cup cooked quinoa

CILANTRO-LIME DRESSING:

1 tablespoon freshly squeezed lime juice

$1^1/2$ teaspoons chopped fresh cilantro

$1^1/2$ teaspoons grated parmesan cheese

$1/2$ teaspoon agave

1 tablespoon pepitas (green pumpkin seeds)

> You can broil and steam the pepper as in the directions below. Or you can char it on a grill or directly over a gas stove's flame (use metal tongs to hold it and turn it slowly). Once all of the skin is blackened, put the pepper in a paper bag and fold the bag closed. The skin will steam a bit in the warm bag, and when the pepper is cool it'll be easy to peel the char away.

Preheat the broiler. Line a baking sheet with foil.

Cut the bell pepper in half lengthwise; discard the stem and seeds. Place the halves, skin sides up, on the lined baking sheet. Broil for 5 to 10 minutes or until charred.

Carefully fold the foil tightly around the pepper halves and let stand for 10 minutes.

Peel the skin off the pepper by rubbing lightly with a paper towel; chop the pepper. Place it in a bowl along with the kale, chicken, tomatoes, and quinoa.

Blend the dressing ingredients.

Toss the salad with the cilantro-lime dressing.

Nutrition information: 284 calories, 21g protein, 40g carbs, 7g fat, 7g fiber

Greek Burger with Sun-Dried Tomato "Aioli"

Using Greek yogurt as a base lightens up a traditionally heavy (French) sauce. The added twist of flavors—sun-dried tomatoes, kalamata olives, and oregano—continues the Greek theme!

BURGER:

3 ounces lean ground beef

1/2 teaspoon garlic powder

1/4 teaspoon freshly ground black pepper

1 tablespoon chopped fresh parsley

Olive oil spray

1 whole-wheat English muffin, toasted

Handful of arugula

SUN-DRIED TOMATO "AIOLI":

2 tablespoons plain nonfat Greek yogurt

2 oil-packed sun-dried tomatoes, rinsed and chopped

1 tablespoon chopped pitted kalamata olives

1/2 garlic clove, crushed

1/2 teaspoon chopped fresh oregano (or a small pinch of dried oregano)

Mix the beef with the garlic powder, pepper, and parsley. Shape the beef into a patty. Cook over medium-high heat, either in a skillet coated with olive oil spray or on a grill, for at least 4 minutes on each side.

In the meantime, mix all of the "aioli" ingredients. Spread on one or both halves of the English muffin, then top with the arugula, beef patty, and other muffin half.

Nutrition information: 293 calories, 27g protein, 30g carbs, 10g fat, 8g fiber

Cajun Chicken Sandwich

The spicy marinated chicken is the star of this dish—you might want to use the bun or toasted bread to mop up all of the juices and flavor left on your plate!

MARINADE:

1 teaspoon olive oil

1/4 cup low-sodium crushed tomatoes

1/2 garlic clove, crushed

1/8 teaspoon ground cumin

1/8 teaspoon chili powder

1/8 teaspoon dried oregano

Pinch of cayenne pepper

SANDWICH:

4 ounces boneless, skinless chicken breast

1/2 whole-grain bun or 1 slice of Ezekiel bread, toasted

Condiments (sliced tomato, cucumber, mustard, Greek yogurt, etc.)

Handful of mixed greens

Preheat the oven to 350°F.

Place all of the marinade ingredients in a zip-top plastic bag. Mix together until well combined.

Add the chicken breast to the bag and massage the marinade into the meat. Refrigerate for 20 to 30 minutes.

Place the chicken and the marinade in a glass baking dish. Bake for 20 to 22 minutes, until the chicken is no longer pink in the center.

Serve open-faced on the toasted bun or bread with condiments of your choice; top with the greens.

Nutrition information: 251 calories, 27g protein, 20g carbs, 8g fat, 5g fiber

Leaving off the top piece of bread in any sandwich is a simple yet meaningful step toward cutting down the carbs and unnecessary calories. In addition, you'll actually taste the sandwich ingredients more if you peel off that starchy top layer. Start going open-faced today!

Beef Chili

The base of a healthy chili is pretty simple—peppers, onions, garlic, cumin, chili powder, and tomatoes (and any other veggies you like). In this case, I used lean beef, but you can certainly substitute ground white turkey or chicken. For an extra metabolism boost, add jalapeño or chiles.

$^1/_2$ teaspoon olive oil

3 ounces lean ground beef

$^1/_2$ cup chopped red bell pepper

$^1/_4$ cup chopped red onion

2 garlic cloves, minced

1 cup chopped zucchini

1 teaspoon chili powder

$^1/_2$ teaspoon ground cumin

1 cup chopped tomatoes

1 cup low-sodium chicken broth

2 cups chopped fresh spinach

2 tablespoons chopped fresh cilantro

Heat the olive oil in a large pot over medium-high heat. Add the beef, bell pepper, onion, and garlic to the pot and sauté for 6 minutes, stirring occasionally.

Stir in the zucchini, chili powder, and cumin; sauté for 1 minute.

Add the tomatoes and broth; bring to a boil. Reduce the heat to medium-low; cover and simmer for 20 minutes.

Stir in the spinach and cilantro. Cook uncovered for 5 more minutes.

Nutrition information: 281 calories, 25g protein, 29g carbs, 10g fat, 8g fiber

Turkey Clean Joes

To "clean up" a sloppy Joe, I added finely diced veggies and took out all the excess salt and fat. You're still going to need a napkin, though!

1 teaspoon olive oil

3 ounces ground white meat turkey

1/4 cup chopped red onion

1 garlic clove, crushed

1/3 cup finely chopped green bell pepper

1/3 cup finely chopped broccoli

1/2 cup tomato sauce

Pinch of chili powder

Pinch of ground cumin

Pinch of dried oregano

Pinch of freshly ground black pepper

1/2 whole-grain bun, toasted

Handful of mixed salad greens

You know those sloppy Joes you concoct from a packet of "Sloppy Joe" seasoning? They are literally sloppy (which is not something I hold against them) but also "dirty" in the sense that they are loaded with salt and chemically enhanced seasoning. Skinny Meals are about *clean* eating—consuming foods that are from nature, not rigorously processed, and not overloaded with saturated fats.

Heat a medium skillet over medium-high heat and coat with the olive oil. Add the turkey, onion, and garlic. Cook for 10 minutes, stirring occasionally and breaking the turkey into crumbles.

Add the bell pepper, broccoli, tomato sauce, and spices. Reduce the heat to medium-low and simmer until the sauce is thickened, about 10 minutes.

Serve on the bun, topped with mixed greens.

Nutrition information: 287 calories, 27g protein, 30g carbs, 8g fat, 7g fiber

Tomato Turkey Meatball Soup

Once you make a batch of meatballs, the culinary world is your oyster. Put them in soups, quesadillas, open-faced sandwiches, and even omelets if you're feeling adventurous.

2 cooked Turkey Meatballs (see sidebar), quartered

1/2 cup Marinara (page 110)

1/3 cup shredded zucchini

2 cups low-sodium chicken broth

1 cup chopped fresh spinach

2 tablespoons chopped fresh basil

Pinch of crushed red pepper

Combine the meatballs, marinara, zucchini, and broth in a pot. Bring to a boil, then reduce the heat. Simmer, uncovered, for 10 minutes.

Add the spinach, basil, and crushed red pepper. Simmer, stirring, until the spinach is wilted, just a minute or two.

Nutrition information: 280 calories, 29g protein, 23g carbs, 9g fat, 5g fiber

Tempeh Burrito

Don't be intimidated by the word "tempeh." It's a soy-based product that contains six times more fiber than tofu and you can buy it in almost any grocery store. It's an easy-to-cook ingredient you can reach for when you're adhering to Rule 12—making one full day of the week meatless.

 Meatless day option!

1/3 cup tempeh, coarsely chopped

1/2 teaspoon olive oil

1 garlic clove, minced

1/4 teaspoon smoked paprika

1/2 teaspoon chili powder

1/4 cup low-sodium vegetable broth

1/4 cup tomato sauce

1 cup chopped kale

1/4 cup shredded zucchini

1/3 cup coarsely chopped cauliflower

1 Ezekiel tortilla

Steam the tempeh for 5 minutes. Set aside on a paper towel.

Heat a medium skillet over medium-high heat and coat it with the olive oil. Add the tempeh and garlic and cook through, approximately 4 minutes, stirring occasionally.

Add the paprika, chili powder, broth, tomato sauce, kale, zucchini, and cauliflower. Cover and simmer for 6 to 8 minutes, stirring occasionally, to allow the vegetables to soften and the sauce to thicken slightly.

Spoon everything onto the tortilla and wrap it like a burrito.

Nutrition information: 281 calories, 17g protein, 35g carbs, 10g fat, 7g fiber

Garbanzo Falafel Salad

Biting into a crispy falafel is always such a treat until I remember that they are crispy thanks to a nice swim in a bath of frying oil. Baking almost always works as an alternative to deep-frying, and in this instance it works wonderfully. The almond butter helps bind the chickpea mixture, ensuring that the falafel balls keep their shape when baked.

 Meatless day option!

Olive oil spray

2 tablespoons chopped fresh parsley

3/4 cup chopped fresh spinach

1/3 cup canned garbanzo beans (chickpeas), rinsed and drained

1/2 garlic clove, crushed

1 1/2 teaspoons unsweetened almond butter

1 teaspoon freshly squeezed lemon juice

Pinch of ground cumin

1 tablespoon ground flaxseed

2 cups mixed greens

TZATZIKI:

1/3 cup plain 2% fat Greek yogurt

1 Persian cucumber, finely chopped

1 teaspoon freshly squeezed lemon juice

1 teaspoon chopped fresh mint

1 teaspoon chopped fresh parsley

Preheat the oven to 375°F. Coat a baking sheet with olive oil spray.

Put the parsley, spinach, garbanzo beans, garlic, almond butter, lemon juice, and cumin in the bowl of a food processor; pulse until well combined.

Transfer to a bowl and mix in the flaxseed. Shape the mixture into small falafel balls.

Place the falafels on the baking sheet and bake for 5 minutes. Flip and bake for an additional 5 to 7 minutes, until golden brown on both sides.

In the meantime, in a small bowl, mix all of the tzatziki ingredients.

Serve the falafel on the mixed greens with a dollop of tzatziki.

Nutrition information: 281 calories, 17g protein, 40g carbs, 10g fat, 9g fiber

Spanish Salad with Cucumber Pico de Gallo

Cucumbers are water-based veggies—light in calories but high in vitamin C and vitamin K, and if you keep the peel on, fiber. Yah, Rule 5! Also, feel free to dial down the heat by reducing the amount of chipotle pepper in this recipe.

To make this a meatless meal, swap the chicken for beans—black, garbanzo, kidney, pinto, or cannellini.

CUCUMBER PICO DE GALLO:

$1/2$ cup Pico de Gallo (page 45)

1 Persian cucumber, finely diced

2 tablespoons diced avocado

SALAD:

4 ounces roasted boneless, skinless chicken breast, shredded (or $1/3$ cup beans)

1 cup roasted veggies

$1/2$ chipotle pepper (canned in adobo), chopped

Mix the pico de gallo with the cucumber and avocado.

Toss the chicken (or beans), veggies, and chipotle with the cucumber pico de gallo.

Nutrition information: 265 calories, 28g protein, 36g carbs, 8g fat, 8g fiber
Meatless option: 230 calories, 11g protein, 49g carbs, 6g fat, 13g fiber

Cucumbers come in a number of varieties—from pickling cukes to English seedless to the small, thin-skinned variety that I love: Persian cucumbers. I snack on Persian cucumbers all day long! When added to a salad or, in this instance, my pico de gallo, they add both nutrients and texture.

Beet Tabbouleh

I love beets, even though I don't recommend eating a lot of them because of their high sugar concentration. Still, you need to have one go-to recipe for getting them on your menu, and this is going to be it!

1 small beet, including greens, rinsed

1 Persian cucumber, diced

1 1/2 teaspoons chopped fresh parsley

2 teaspoons chopped fresh mint

1 scallion, white and green parts, thinly sliced

1 tablespoon freshly squeezed lemon juice

1 cup chopped fresh spinach or arugula

1/2 teaspoon olive oil

4 ounces roasted boneless, skinless chicken breast, cut into cubes

1/4 cup cooked quinoa

Preheat the oven to 450°F.

Remove the greens from the beet and finely chop them. Set aside.

Wrap the beet tightly in two layers of foil. Place it in the oven and bake for 35 to 40 minutes.

Remove the packet from the oven and allow it to cool for 20 minutes. Unwrap the beet and peel by rubbing the skin off with a paper towel. Chop the beet into cubes.

Toss with the remaining ingredients, including the beet greens.

> Beets are full of wonderful anti-inflammatory properties and vitamins. Plus, beets' natural sweetness is pretty irresistible. This single-serving recipe calls for one small beet, including its greens, but just that one beet provides the right hit of taste and color.

Nutrition information: 258 calories, 27g protein, 31g carbs, 7g fat, 4g fiber

Spaghetti Squash Pad Thai

Pad Thai is a rice noodle dish that's usually drenched in peanut sauce and loaded with carbs. Cooked spaghetti squash really looks like thin noodles, and if you steam the vegetables and chicken in broth, you strip out the fat!

Olive oil spray

3 ounces boneless, skinless chicken breast, cut into strips

1 cup shredded mixed vegetables (zucchini, broccoli, cabbage, carrots)

1 tablespoon Bragg Liquid Aminos

2 tablespoons low-sodium chicken broth

1 1/2 teaspoons unsweetened almond butter

1/2 teaspoon Sriracha

1/2 teaspoon minced garlic

1/4 teaspoon minced fresh ginger

1/2 teaspoon agave

1 teaspoon rice wine vinegar

1 1/2 cups prepared spaghetti squash (see sidebar)

Fresh cilantro leaves, for garnish

Lots of people never experience the fabulousness of spaghetti squash because they are intimidated by its very hard skin. Be afraid no more! Once you cut the squash in half (which takes some elbow grease and a sharp knife) and scrape out the seeds, this couldn't be an easier vegetable to cook: just immerse the halves in boiling water in a large pot and let it boil for 15 to 20 minutes, then drain and let cool for a few minutes. You know the squash is done when you drag a fork through the flesh and it falls off in long, spaghetti-like strips.

Coat a medium skillet with olive oil spray and heat over medium-high heat. Add the chicken and cook for 4 minutes, stirring occasionally. Add the veggies and cook for another 5 minutes, stirring along the way.

In the meantime, whisk the Bragg Aminos, broth, almond butter, Sriracha, garlic, ginger, agave, and vinegar in a small bowl.

Pour the sauce into the skillet and heat through. Add the spaghetti squash and toss.

Garnish with cilantro and serve.

Nutrition information: 240 calories, 22g protein, 28g carbs, 8g fat, 7g fiber

Smoked Salmon "Tea" Wraps

These wraps are like little finger sandwiches served for tea, and they are a great substitute for the bagel, cream cheese, and smoked salmon you *used to* reach for. Feel free to add tomato, red onion, or any other vegetable on top.

5 to 8 thin slices of cucumber

1/4 cup plain 2% fat Greek yogurt

1/2 teaspoon fresh dill

1/4 teaspoon fresh chives

1/2 teaspoon freshly squeezed lemon juice

1 Ezekiel tortilla

3 ounces smoked salmon

1/2 cup arugula

In a small bowl, stir the cucumber, yogurt, dill, chives, and lemon juice.

Spread the mixture on the tortilla. Top with the salmon and arugula.

Wrap like a burrito.

Nutrition information: 298 calories, 28g protein, 27g carbs, 9g fat, 6g fiber

Cream cheese needs to be a thing of your past, OK? But that doesn't mean you have to live without a thick, creamy topping for this recipe. Here's a tip: Line a small colander with a clean cloth or 5 or 6 folded paper towels and set it over a bowl. Place the Greek yogurt in the colander, cover with plastic wrap, and refrigerate overnight. The liquid will slowly be absorbed by or drain through the towels and the next day it will be thick, tangy, and, after mixed thoroughly, as creamy as cream cheese!

Garbanzo Bean Salad

Garbanzo beans (high in fiber) and avocado (healthy fat) mash up beautifully with herbs, giving you a great alternative to mayo in your summertime salads.

1/3 cup garbanzo beans, drained and rinsed

1/4 cup diced avocado

1 teaspoon freshly squeezed lemon juice

1 tablespoon chopped fresh parsley

1/2 teaspoon chopped fresh chives

3 hard-boiled large egg whites, chopped

2 cups mixed salad greens

1/2 slice Ezekiel bread, toasted

Coarsely mash the beans with the avocado, lemon juice, parsley, and chives. Fold in the egg whites.

Pile the bean mixture on top of the greens. Dip the bread into the mash and/or spread some on the bread.

Nutrition information: 280 calories, 20g protein, 36g carbs, 8g fat, 10g fiber

Turkey and Fig Jam Panini

The inspiration here is a pizza with bacon, blackberries, and rosemary that a friend told me she had at a restaurant. I immediately tried the rosemary/fruit combination at home myself. What a great and delicious surprise! Make your own sandwich spread using whatever berry or fruit you find in the market. Here I combined figs and rosemary with tangy balsamic to make the low-calorie and low-sugar "jam."

FIG "JAM":

2 fresh figs, quartered

1/4 teaspoon chopped fresh rosemary leaves

1/2 teaspoon balsamic vinegar

TURKEY PANINI:

2 slices of whole-grain bread

2 tablespoons grated low-fat mozzarella

4 ounces sliced low-sodium deli turkey

Handful of arugula

Olive oil spray

In a small bowl, mash the figs with the rosemary and balsamic.

Spread the jam on both slices of bread. Layer the cheese, turkey, and arugula between the 2 slices.

Heat a small skillet over medium-high heat and spray with olive oil. Grill the sandwich for 3 minutes on each side.

Nutrition information: 284 calories, 23g protein, 33g carbs, 8g fat, 8g fiber

Irish Flag Flying

Green broccoli, white yogurt, orange sweet potato—it's the Irish flag (and the Indian, and others, of course). However you eat this concoction—with the toppings piled into the potato or everything diced up on your plate—you're getting good carbs, protein, and vegetables, the perfect combination to keep you full for hours.

1 small sweet potato, cooked

2 cups broccoli, steamed

Dollop of plain nonfat Greek yogurt

4 ounces roasted boneless, skinless chicken breast

Cut open the sweet potato and top with the broccoli and a dollop of Greek yogurt.

Serve the chicken alongside, or cut it up and pile it on the potato as well.

Nutrition information: 267 calories, 29g protein, 34g carbs, 5g fat, 8g fiber

This is a lunch you can throw together from precooked ingredients. If you've followed the make-ahead tips for the week, you'll have some roasted chicken breast and perhaps even some steamed broccoli ready to go. All you have to do now is poke four or five holes in a small sweet potato and microwave it on high power for four to five minutes. Pile it all together on a plate and voilà—a well-balanced "lean lunch."

Salmon Tacos with Avocado Crema

A dollop of crema is a welcome hit of cool in your mouth when you're eating something spicy. But traditional crema is not going to help you lose weight. Make it out of avocado—a healthy, nourishing fat—and nonfat Greek yogurt, which adds a silkiness and tang, and you can spoon it on without worry!

SALMON:

2 teaspoons freshly squeezed lime juice

1/4 teaspoon ground cumin

4 ounces wild-caught salmon

Olive oil spray

2 big lettuce leaves

SLAW:

1 tablespoon plain nonfat Greek yogurt

1/2 teaspoon red wine vinegar

1 tablespoon chopped fresh cilantro

1/2 cup shredded red cabbage

AVOCADO CREMA:

1/4 cup mashed avocado

2 tablespoons plain nonfat Greek yogurt

1 teaspoon freshly squeezed lime juice

Pinch of cayenne

> When purchasing seafood, spend the extra money for "wild caught," which means fish that live in their natural habitat. "Farm-raised" fish are produced in a man-made, crowded space, so the fish are growing, nurturing, and feeding off of each other's waste. A wild-caught fish is a cleaner product.

Massage the lime juice and cumin into the salmon so that the fish is evenly coated. Cover with plastic wrap and refrigerate for 10 to 15 minutes.

Meanwhile, combine the yogurt, red wine vinegar, and cilantro in a small bowl. Add the red cabbage and toss.

In another small bowl, mix the avocado crema ingredients.

Coat a skillet with olive oil spray and heat over medium-high heat. Add the salmon and sear for 4 to 5 minutes on each side. When done, cut into chunks and place in the lettuce cups. Top with slaw and avocado crema.

Nutrition information: 215 calories, 26g protein, 10g carbs, 9g fat, 9g fiber

Lentil Salad with Herb Dressing

Lentils are an incredible source of protein and fiber. You can now buy them pre-cooked in many stores, but if you cook them at home, you can enhance their flavor by replacing the water called for in the directions with broth. You can also add herbs—a stem of thyme, or a pinch of some of your favorite dried seasonings—to bring up the flavor even more.

HERB DRESSING:

1 teaspoon finely chopped fresh oregano (or $1/2$ teaspoon dried)

2 teaspoons chopped fresh parsley

1 tablespoon freshly squeezed lemon juice

$1 1/2$ teaspoons minced shallot

1 teaspoon Dijon mustard

$1/2$ teaspoon olive oil

1 teaspoon white wine vinegar

LENTIL SALAD:

$1/3$ cup cooked lentils

1 Persian cucumber, diced

$1/4$ cup halved cherry tomatoes

2 cups chopped mixed salad greens

4 pitted kalamata olives, quartered

3 ounces roasted boneless, skinless chicken breast, cut into cubes

In a food processor, blend the dressing ingredients.

Toss the lentils, cucumber, tomatoes, mixed greens, olives, and chicken in the herb dressing.

Nutrition information: 272 calories, 25g protein, 33g carbs, 9g fat, 8g fiber

Cajun Bowl

The "Cajun" heat in this dish comes from the Tabasco. If you want to turn this into an "Italian Bowl," swap the Tabasco, cilantro, and dried seasonings for crushed red pepper, basil, and parsley.

To make this a meatless meal, ditch the chicken and add more beans.

CAJUN DRESSING:

1 teaspoon olive oil

1 teaspoon red wine vinegar

1/2 teaspoon Tabasco

1 tablespoon chopped fresh cilantro

Pinch of chili powder

Pinch of smoked paprika

Pinch of ground cumin

CAJUN BOWL:

3 ounces roasted boneless, skinless chicken breast, cut into cubes

1 cup chopped bell peppers

1 plum tomato, chopped

1/4 cup black beans, drained and rinsed (plus another 1/3 cup for meatless option)

2 cups shredded lettuce

Whisk the dressing ingredients in a medium bowl. Toss with the chicken, bell peppers, tomato, and black beans.

Serve on top of a bed of lettuce.

Nutrition information: 255 calories, 24g protein, 27g carbs, 9g fat, 8g fiber
Meatless option: 270 calories, 14g protein, 42g carbs, 6g fat, 13g fiber

Harpersized Salad

You don't need egg yolks, cups of oil, or mayonnaise to make a memorable salad dressing. The key to an outstanding, guilt-free dressing is to use just enough olive oil to get the proper amount of fat in your meal, and then flavor it up with vinegar or broth and any herb combo you want.

LEMON-BASIL DRESSING:

1 tablespoon freshly squeezed lemon juice

1 tablespoon chopped fresh basil

$1/2$ garlic clove, crushed

1 teaspoon olive oil

1 tablespoon white wine vinegar
   (or apple cider vinegar)

SALAD:

$1/4$ cup chopped red bell pepper

$1/4$ cup shredded carrot

$1/3$ cup shredded yellow squash

$1/2$ cup chopped broccoli

4 asparagus spears, steamed and chopped

$1/2$ cup shredded red cabbage

4 ounces roasted boneless, skinless chicken breast, shredded

In a food processor, blend the dressing ingredients.

Toss the salad ingredients with the lemon-basil dressing.

Nutrition information: 221 calories, 26g protein, 16g carbs, 8g fat, 6g fiber

In *The Skinny Rules* I introduced you to a salad or vegetable eating technique I like to call "Harpersizing." Instead of portion *control,* this one is about portion *out of control!* When it comes to vegetables, you just can't go wrong—pile them on your plate, as in this salad. Take advantage of their high-fiber, low-calorie goodness! You cannot get fat by eating vegetables, so load 'em up and then add this guilt-free dressing to enhance their deliciousness.

Nachos with Chipotle-Lime Cream

The problem with restaurant nachos, aside from the cheese and sour cream, is that without realizing it, you've eaten the equivalent of four fried tortillas. Control your portion by making your own chips out of one baked tortilla.

You can make this one meatless by using beans—black, kidney, pinto—or even steamed tempeh in place of the turkey.

1 Ezekiel tortilla

Olive oil spray

1 teaspoon olive oil

3 ounces ground white turkey (or 1/3 cup beans or steamed tempeh)

1/4 cup chopped red onion

1 garlic clove, crushed

1/2 teaspoon dried oregano

Pinch of crushed red pepper

Pinch of freshly ground black pepper

1/2 cup shredded zucchini

2 plum tomatoes, chopped

CHIPOTLE-LIME CREAM:

1 tablespoon chopped chipotle pepper (canned in adobo)

1 tablespoon chopped fresh cilantro

1 tablespoon freshly squeezed lime juice

1/4 cup plain nonfat Greek yogurt

Preheat the oven to 375°F.

Coat both sides of the tortilla with olive oil spray, then cut into 1-inch squares. Place on a baking sheet in a single layer and bake for 5 minutes. Flip the tortilla pieces and bake for an additional 5 minutes, or until crispy.

In the meantime, heat the olive oil in a skillet over medium heat. Add the turkey (or beans or tempeh), onion, and garlic; sauté for 8 minutes, stirring occasionally and breaking the turkey into crumbles.

Add the oregano, crushed red pepper, black pepper, zucchini, and tomatoes and cook for another 4 minutes.

In the meantime, mix all of the chipotle-lime cream ingredients together.

Place the turkey mixture on the baked tortilla chips.

Drizzle the nachos with the chipotle-lime cream or use as a dip.

Nutrition information: 315 calories, 30g protein, 29g carbs, 9g fat, 6g fiber
Meatless option: 285 calories, 16g protein, 43g carbs, 6g fat, 10g fiber

Roasted Eggplant Salad

Eggplant is an excellent source of fiber and promotes a healthy digestive system, but because it contains a lot of water, it takes the proper preparation to keep it from turning into a rubbery disaster. Salting the cut eggplant and then letting it sit is a good way to extract the water, but it's also a great way to add unnecessary salt to your diet! Rule 16 solution? Cook the eggplant at a high temperature (roasting) to dehydrate it.

1 cup chopped eggplant, unpeeled

1/2 teaspoon olive oil

1/4 cup minced red onion

1/2 garlic clove, thinly sliced

1 to 2 tablespoons balsamic vinegar

1 tablespoon crumbled feta cheese

4 ounces roasted boneless, skinless chicken breast, cut into cubes

1 cup arugula

1 cup mixed salad greens

Preheat the oven to 400°F.

Toss the eggplant, olive oil, red onion, and garlic in a small baking dish and place it in the oven. Bake for 10 minutes, then stir. Bake for another 10 minutes.

Add the balsamic vinegar and feta. Stir and bake for an additional 4 to 5 minutes.

Add the chicken and toss with the eggplant; serve on top of the arugula and greens.

Nutrition information: 221 calories, 27g protein, 12g carbs, 9g fat, 5g fiber

Sesame Bowl

The sesame oil, Bragg Liquid Aminos, and broth combine here to approximate your favorite Asian takeout flavors, without slathering any of the nutritious vegetables with highly salty soy sauce or sugary teriyaki sauce.

Make this meatless by using vegetable broth instead of chicken broth.

Many vegetarians and vegans use Bragg Liquid Aminos to help replace some of the amino acids they miss by staying away from animal proteins. Bragg's is also naturally gluten-free, so it has become a popular alternative to soy sauce (which often contains gluten). It's not terribly low in sodium, though, so don't go overboard!

1 teaspoon toasted sesame oil

5 crimini mushrooms, chopped

5 asparagus spears, cut into fourths

1 cup broccoli, coarsely chopped

1 tablespoon Bragg Liquid Aminos

1/4 cup low-sodium chicken broth
(or vegetable broth for a meatless meal)

Crushed red pepper, as much as your heart desires

1 cup chopped Swiss (or rainbow) chard, stems removed

1 cup chopped fresh spinach

1/3 cup cooked quinoa

Heat the sesame oil in a large skillet over medium heat. Add the mushrooms and sauté for 6 minutes, stirring occasionally.

Add the asparagus, broccoli, Bragg Aminos, broth, and crushed red pepper. Sauté for another 6 minutes. Toss in the chard and spinach and cook until wilted.

Place the quinoa in a bowl and top with the veggies.

Nutrition information: 249 calories, 17g protein, 39g carbs, 7g fat, 12g fiber

Banh Mi Chicken Salad

Banh mi is Vietnamese for baguette and a street vendor sandwich of the same name. With this tangy Vietnamese-inspired dressing, you'll hardly miss the bread in this salad version of the traditional street food.

DRESSING:

1 tablespoon rice wine vinegar

1 teaspoon agave

1 teaspoon olive oil

1/2 teaspoon toasted sesame oil

SALAD:

1 tablespoon finely chopped fresh cilantro

1/2 small jalapeño pepper, seeded and minced

4 ounces roasted boneless, skinless chicken breast, shredded

1/4 cup shredded carrots

1 radish, thinly sliced

2 cups mixed salad greens

Mix all of the dressing ingredients together in a medium bowl.

Add all of the salad ingredients and toss with the dressing.

Nutrition information: 227 calories, 24g protein, 13g carbs, 10g fat, 4g fiber

Chicken, Nectarine, and Zucchini Skewers

You can skewer anything you please, as long as the cooking time for each item doesn't vary too drastically. Make sure your ingredients are cut to the same size or thickness to avoid uneven cooking. Also, if using wooden skewers, soaking them first is important so they don't burn.

MARINADE:

1 teaspoon olive oil

1 teaspoon agave

2 teaspoons red wine vinegar

1 teaspoon Dijon mustard

SKEWERS:

4 ounces boneless, skinless chicken breast, cut into cubes

1 nectarine (or peach), cut into cubes

1 small zucchini, cut into $1/2$-inch rounds

2 cups mixed salad greens

Mix the marinade ingredients in a zip-top bag. Add the chicken and marinate in the refrigerator for 30 to 40 minutes.

In the meantime, soak three wooden skewers in water for the same amount of time.

Skewer the chicken, nectarine, and zucchini, alternating the order until done.

Grill or sauté the skewers over medium-high heat for 3 minutes on each side, for a total of 12 minutes, or until the chicken is cooked through.

Serve alongside the mixed greens.

Nutrition information: 283 calories, 26g protein, 32g carbs, 8g fat, 7g fiber

Moroccan Beef with Squash

This stew celebrates Moroccan flavors with a healthy twist. Adding kale will up the iron and nutritional value, so throw it in your meal anytime you want.

Olive oil spray

1/4 cup chopped yellow onion

1 garlic clove, crushed

4 ounces lean beef (top sirloin, tenderloin), cubed

1/3 cup cubed butternut squash

1/8 teaspoon cinnamon

1/4 teaspoon paprika

1/4 teaspoon ground cumin

1/2 teaspoon curry powder

1 cup canned diced tomatoes, drained

1 cup low-sodium chicken broth

1 cup chopped kale

Moroccan food is loaded with spices and, oftentimes, dried fruit like golden raisins or apricots. My issue with dried fruits is that you eat a whole lot more of them than you would the fresh fruit. One grape and one raisin have the same calorie count—about 3.5 calories—but if you eat one cup of grapes you'll eat about 60 calories. One cup of raisins? Four hundred!

Coat a heavy pot with olive oil spray and heat over medium heat. Add the onion and garlic and sauté for 5 minutes, stirring occasionally. Stir in the beef and cook for another 5 minutes.

Add the butternut squash, cinnamon, paprika, cumin, and curry powder. Mix until everything is coated.

Add the tomatoes and broth. Bring to a boil, then reduce the heat, cover, and simmer for 15 to 20 minutes, or until the squash is fork-tender.

Stir in the kale and cook until wilted.

Nutrition information: 296 calories, 30g protein, 27g carbs, 9g fat, 7g fiber

Lemon-Basil Chicken Salad

The combination of soft tomato and avocado and crisp cucumber and arugula is a great texture pairing. Arugula's peppery bite is also a nice complement to the blander avocado.

1/4 avocado, cubed

1/2 cup halved cherry tomatoes

1/2 shallot, thinly sliced

5 basil leaves, cut into a chiffonade

1 teaspoon freshly squeezed lemon juice

1/2 cup coarsely chopped arugula

1 cup mixed salad greens

1 Persian cucumber, sliced

4 ounces roasted boneless, skinless chicken breast, cut into cubes

Lightly toss the avocado, tomatoes, shallot, and basil leaves with the lemon juice.

Place on a bed of arugula and mixed greens. Top with the cucumber and chicken.

Nutrition information: 231 calories, 25g protein, 21g carbs, 10g fat, 5g fiber

Greens Minestrone Soup

Soups are not only comforting for the soul, they're also good for your body. You can pack in a ton of veggies and because you have to eat it with a spoon, you'll naturally slow down, allowing your body to recognize that you're full when you really are.

1 teaspoon olive oil

1/4 cup chopped yellow onion

1 garlic clove, thinly sliced

2 ounces boneless, skinless chicken breast, cut into cubes

1/2 teaspoon dried thyme

1 bay leaf

2 plum tomatoes, diced

1/4 teaspoon crushed red pepper

2 cups low-sodium chicken broth

1/3 cup cannellini beans, drained and rinsed

2 cups coarsely chopped greens (collard, kale, chard, spinach, etc.)

1 teaspoon red wine vinegar

2 teaspoons shaved parmesan cheese (optional)

Heat the olive oil in a soup pot over medium-high heat. Add the onion and garlic; sauté for 5 minutes, stirring occasionally.

Add the chicken and cook for 2 minutes, stirring.

Add the thyme and bay leaf. Stir and cook for 2 more minutes.

> Greens reduce dramatically—two cups wilt down to almost nothing. It's important to add your greens to the soup last because the longer they stew, the more nutrients are lost in the cooking process.

Pour in the tomatoes, crushed red pepper, broth, and beans. Reduce the heat and simmer for 20 minutes.

Turn off the heat and remove the bay leaf. Add the greens and vinegar; stir until slightly wilted.

Sprinkle with parmesan, if desired.

Nutrition information: 282 calories, 24g protein, 32g carbs, 8g fat, 8g fiber

THINNER DINNERS

Rule 7 dictates that your carbohydrate chowing cannot extend to your dinner. Remember the mantra? Lean and green for dinner, people! As I hope you'll agree once you explore these thirty-five dinner options, however, lean and green is oh-so-delicious and satisfying. You're going to go to bed a little hungry (Rule 18) not because you're denying yourself at dinner but rather because you won't be snacking afterward. And if you're eating any of these lean and green meals that follow, you're not going to want to snack before bed anyway!

Pan-Seared Salmon with Zucchini and Yellow Squash

With the pink salmon and the green, red, and yellow of the vegetables, this is a colorful and fancy-looking dish. Don't let it fool you, though—it's supremely easy to make!

1 teaspoon olive oil

1/2 cup sliced zucchini, cut into 1/2-inch rounds

1 cup sliced yellow squash, cut into 1/2-inch rounds

1 garlic clove, crushed

1/2 cup halved cherry tomatoes

1/4 teaspoon crushed red pepper

1 teaspoon fresh thyme leaves

4 ounces wild-caught salmon fillet

1/2 lemon, thinly sliced

Preheat the oven to 350°F. Place a piece of foil on a baking sheet. Lightly coat with 1/2 teaspoon of the olive oil.

In a bowl, toss the zucchini and yellow squash with the garlic, tomatoes, crushed red pepper, thyme, and remaining 1/2 teaspoon olive oil.

Place the vegetables on the foil. Top with the salmon. Place the lemon slices on the salmon in a single layer.

Too many people are intimidated by cooking fish, when all you really need to do is sear it on one side, then flip it over. It's really that simple. I'm taking things only one step further here—sear it first to lock in all the great flavors and then bake it to make sure it's evenly cooked through.

Bake for 15 to 20 minutes, or until the salmon is cooked through.

Nutrition information: 220 calories, 29g protein, 14g carbs, 6g fat, 5g fiber

Spaghetti Squash Casserole

Spaghetti squash absorbs flavors easily but holds its texture well, even when cooked again (see page 84 for advice on cutting and cooking it). By replacing a heavy cheese (what you might expect in a casserole) with tangy cottage cheese, you get a simple and delicious lunchtime concoction.

If you want to make this your meatless day dinner, add extra veggies in place of the turkey.

Olive oil spray
4 ounces ground white turkey
1 garlic clove, crushed
1 cup roasted veggies
1 cup cooked spaghetti squash
1/2 cup Marinara (see sidebar)
1/4 cup low-fat cottage cheese

Preheat the oven to 350°F. Coat a small baking dish with olive oil spray.

Coat a small skillet with olive oil spray and heat over medium heat. Add the turkey and garlic. Sauté for 7 minutes, stirring occasionally, breaking the turkey into crumbles.

In a medium bowl, mix the remaining ingredients. When the turkey is done, add it to the bowl, toss to combine, then pour everything into the prepared baking dish.

Bake for 25 minutes.

> **MY MARINARA**
>
> From my book *Jumpstart to Skinny,* here is my simple marinara recipe:
>
> 1 tablespoon extra-virgin olive oil
> 1 small yellow onion, chopped
> 2 garlic cloves, crushed
> 1 cup low-sodium vegetable broth
> 1 28-ounce can low-sodium crushed tomatoes
> 1 bay leaf
> 1/4 cup coarsely chopped fresh basil
>
> Heat the olive oil in a medium pot. Sauté the onion in the oil until translucent, about 10 minutes. Add the garlic and stir. Add the broth, tomatoes, and bay leaf. Simmer, uncovered, over low heat until the sauce thickens, about 1 hour. Remove the bay leaf, stir in the basil, and voilà—delicious! Store in an airtight container in the refrigerator.

Nutrition information: 299 calories, 30g protein, 29g carbs, 9g fat, 5g fiber

Chicken Curry over Cauliflower "Rice"

Cauliflower might be the most diverse vegetable on the planet. Plus, despite its bland color, it packs more vitamin C than citrus fruits and more omega-3s than some fish. You can also convert it into mashed "potatoes" or "couscous," but here we'll use it as a substitute for rice, which is what you'd usually get with a curry dish.

To make this a meatless meal, substitute steamed tempeh for the chicken.

Olive oil spray

4 ounces boneless, skinless chicken breast, cut into cubes (or 1/3 cup tempeh)

1/2 teaspoon freshly grated ginger

1 teaspoon red curry paste

1/4 cup "lite" coconut milk

1/2 cup low-sodium chicken broth

1 cup chopped fresh spinach

1 cup chopped kale

2 tablespoons chopped fresh basil

1 cup coarsely chopped cauliflower

Coat a skillet with olive oil spray and heat over medium heat. Add the chicken (or tempeh) and cook for 5 minutes, stirring occasionally.

Add the ginger and curry paste. Stir until the chicken is coated. Cook for 3 minutes.

Pour in the coconut milk and broth. Bring to a boil, then reduce the heat. Cover and simmer for 10 minutes.

Add the spinach, kale, and basil. Stir until wilted.

Place the raw cauliflower in a food processor and pulse until it is like rice. Serve the curry over "rice."

Nutrition information: 222 calories, 28g protein, 17g carbs, 7g fat, 5g fiber
Meatless option: 219 calories, 16g protein, 22g carbs, 9g fat, 6g fiber

Beef Stew over Cauliflower "Couscous"

See what I did here? By processing the cauliflower for just a bit longer than you did to create "rice" (see page 111), you can create couscous. Cauliflower is a chameleon vegetable!

You can make this recipe meatless by substituting tempeh for the cubed beef.

Olive oil spray

1/4 cup chopped onion

1 garlic clove, crushed

4 ounces boneless chuck roast, trimmed and cut into cubes (or 1/3 cup tempeh)

1/4 teaspoon black pepper

2 cups fat-free, low-sodium chicken broth

1 cup chopped plum tomato

2 oil-packed sun-dried tomatoes, rinsed and thinly sliced

1/2 teaspoon chopped fresh oregano

1/2 teaspoon chopped fresh thyme

1 bay leaf

4 crimini mushrooms, quartered

1 tablespoon chopped fresh parsley

1 cup coarsely chopped cauliflower

Heat a soup pot over medium-high heat and generously coat with olive oil spray. Add the onion and garlic. Sauté for 5 minutes, stirring occasionally. Transfer the onion and garlic to a small bowl and set aside.

Sprinkle the beef with the pepper and add it to the pan. Sauté the meat for 6 minutes, browning it on all sides. When the meat is cooked through, remove it from the pan and set aside.

Add the broth to the pot and bring to a boil, scraping the bits on the bottom of the pot with a wooden spoon. Add the plum and sun-dried tomatoes, oregano, thyme, and bay leaf. Reduce the heat and simmer for 5 minutes.

Return the meat, onion, and garlic to the pot. Cover and simmer for 20 minutes.

Stir in the mushrooms. Cook for another 15 minutes, uncovered. Stir in the parsley. Remove the bay leaf.

Meanwhile, place the raw cauliflower in a food processor and pulse until it is like couscous. Serve the stew over the "couscous."

Nutrition information: 294 calories, 33g protein, 24g carbs, 9g fat, 7g fiber

Skinny Shepherd's Pie

I use my cauliflower mash technique here in place of mashed potatoes and lighten the whole thing by using more vegetables than meat.

1 teaspoon olive oil

1/4 cup chopped red onion

4 ounces ground white turkey

1 garlic clove, thinly sliced

1 teaspoon chopped fresh rosemary

1 teaspoon chopped fresh thyme

2 plum tomatoes, chopped

1/2 cup diced red bell pepper

1/2 medium zucchini, cut into 1/2-inch rounds

1 cup chopped cauliflower

1/4 cup low-sodium chicken broth

Olive oil spray

2 teaspoons grated parmesan cheese

Shepherd's pie might be one of the most comforting foods on the planet, and it's especially welcome during the colder months. However, it doesn't need to be covered with buttery mashed potatoes or dripping in meaty gravy to be rich and delicious. The flavors in this skinny version will be every bit as comforting as the fattening "real thing"; the parmesan on top adds a nice salty (but not too salty!) bite.

Preheat the oven to 400°F.

Coat a skillet with the olive oil and heat over medium heat. Add the onion; sauté for 5 minutes, stirring occasionally.

Add the turkey, garlic, rosemary, and thyme and cook for another 5 minutes, breaking the turkey into crumbles.

Add the tomatoes, bell pepper, and zucchini; cook, stirring occasionally, for 4 more minutes.

Meanwhile, place the cauliflower in a small pot with the broth and simmer, covered, for 5 to 7 minutes, until fork-tender.

With a slotted spoon, transfer the warm cauliflower to the bowl of the food processor, reserving the broth. Pulse, adding broth until the desired consistency is reached; it should be the thickness of mashed potatoes.

Coat a small baking dish with olive oil spray. Spread the turkey mixture over the bottom of the dish, then top with the mashed cauliflower and an even sprinkle of parmesan.

Bake for 10 to 12 minutes.

Nutrition information: 288 calories, 32g protein, 22g carbs, 10g fat, 6g fiber

Enchilada Soup

Enchilada soups are typically thickened with cheese and topped with tortilla chips, but here, my green salsa verde keeps things skinny, light, and spicy.

SOUP:

1/2 teaspoon olive oil

2 tablespoons minced white onion

1 garlic clove, crushed

1/4 teaspoon chili powder

4 ounces skinless turkey breast, cut into cubes

1/3 cup chopped red bell pepper

1/2 cup low-sodium canned crushed tomatoes

1 cup low-sodium chicken broth

1/2 cup chopped cauliflower

1 cup chopped kale

ZUCCHINI SALSA:

1/3 cup diced zucchini

1 cup chopped fresh spinach

2 tablespoons chopped white onion

2 tablespoons chopped fresh cilantro

2 tablespoons freshly squeezed lime juice

1/4 cup low-sodium chicken broth

For the soup, heat the olive oil in a skillet over medium heat. Add the onion and garlic and sauté for 4 minutes, stirring occasionally. Add the chili powder, turkey, and bell pepper. Cook for 5 minutes, stirring.

Add the tomatoes, broth, and cauliflower. Bring to a boil, then reduce the heat and cover. Simmer for 15 minutes. Add the kale and stir until wilted.

In the meantime, combine all of the salsa ingredients.

Stir the salsa into the soup and heat through.

> Here's a trick for thickening soup without adding cream or corn-starch (or cheese): simply blend some of it and add it back to the soup pot.

Nutrition information: 269 calories, 33g protein, 22g carbs, 8g fat, 7g fiber

Chinese Chicken Salad

About the only thing that fried wontons add to a salad is fat. Oh, and crunch. So get your crunch from healthier sources—almonds and cabbage.

DRESSING:

1 tablespoon freshly squeezed orange juice

1 teaspoon rice wine vinegar

$1/2$ teaspoon freshly grated ginger

$1/2$ teaspoon agave

1 tablespoon Bragg Liquid Aminos

SALAD:

4 ounces roasted boneless, skinless chicken breast, shredded

4 almonds, sliced

$1/4$ avocado, cut into cubes

$1/2$ cup shredded cabbage

1 scallion, white and light green parts, sliced diagonally

2 cups mixed salad greens

Whisk all of the dressing ingredients in a large bowl.

Add the salad ingredients and toss with the dressing.

Nutrition information: 268 calories, 26g protein, 18g carbs, 12g fat, 7g fiber

As I said in the Do-Ahead Tips section, rice wine vinegar is a great thing to put in your pantry—it's a mellow vinegar but it adds a great Asian taste. If you don't have rice wine vinegar, however, you can definitely use white wine vinegar, which is still mellow.

Pork Loin with Braised Collard Greens

Collard greens are so good for you when they're not boiled in pork juices and butter and served with fried chicken!

1 teaspoon garlic powder

1 teaspoon dried oregano

1 teaspoon ground cumin

1 teaspoon dried thyme

4 ounces pork loin

Olive oil spray

1/4 cup thinly sliced yellow onion

1 garlic clove, thinly sliced

2 plum tomatoes, coarsely chopped

2 cups stemmed and chopped collard greens

Collards, along with other stalk greens like beet greens and dandelion greens, are rich in vitamins, antioxidants, and fiber—a great combination if you're battling your weight (and want to help bolster your health against heart disease and cancer).

In a small bowl, mix the garlic powder, oregano, cumin, and thyme. Pat evenly onto both sides of the pork.

Coat a medium skillet with olive oil spray and heat over medium-high heat. Add the pork; cook for 4 minutes on each side or until done. Remove from the pan and set aside.

Coat the same pan again with olive oil spray and add the onion, garlic, and tomatoes (including juices). Reduce the heat to low and bring to a simmer. Cover and cook for 5 minutes. Add the greens, cover, and simmer for 10 minutes.

Serve with the pork.

Nutrition information: 240 calories, 25g protein, 17g carbs, 7g fat, 7g fiber

Poached Chicken with Lemon, Capers, and Parsley Gremolata

Sounds fancy, but this isn't a complicated dish—poaching chicken is simple and fast, and you can do it ahead and use it in lots of other Skinny Meals ways.

CHICKEN:

1 quart water

1/4 yellow onion

1 celery stalk, cut in half

1 garlic clove, smashed

Fresh herbs (handful of parsley, one sprig of thyme, one sprig of rosemary)

4 ounces boneless, skinless chicken breast

2 cups mixed salad greens

GREMOLATA:

1 1/2 teaspoons capers, rinsed

2 tablespoons coarsely chopped fresh parsley

1/2 garlic clove

1/2 teaspoon grated lemon zest

1 teaspoon olive oil

In a large pot, combine the water, onion, celery, garlic, and herbs. Cover and bring to a slow boil. Reduce the heat and add the chicken. Simmer until cooked through, 10 to 15 minutes, flipping the chicken halfway through.

In the meantime, make the gremolata. Pile the capers, parsley, garlic, and lemon zest on a cutting board and chop finely. Mix with the olive oil.

When the chicken is done, top with the gremolata and serve with mixed greens.

Nutrition information: 194 calories, 25g protein, 10g carbs, 8g fat, 7g fiber

You could use store-bought, low-sodium chicken broth to poach your chicken, but it's even more delicious when you infuse plain old water with herbs and garlic yourself. Poached chicken breast can be cooled and shredded for salads, cubed for lettuce wraps, or served as here, with a side of gremolata. You could also top this chicken with Zucchini Salsa or Pico de Gallo (see pages 115 and 45).

Brussels Sprout Chicken Caesar Salad

Using shaved Brussels sprouts as a component to this salad adds a great texture and will give you added fiber, vitamins, and antioxidants. My light Caesar-inspired dressing helps you cut calories and fat.

10 Brussels sprouts, shredded

1 cup chopped mixed greens or romaine lettuce

4 ounces roasted boneless, skinless chicken breast, shredded

1 tablespoon coarsely chopped almonds

DRESSING:

2 tablespoons plain nonfat Greek yogurt

1 teaspoon freshly squeezed lemon juice

1/4 teaspoon Worcestershire sauce

1/2 garlic clove, crushed

Pinch of freshly ground black pepper

1 tablespoon grated parmesan cheese

1 to 2 teaspoons water to thin

In a medium bowl, toss the Brussels sprouts, lettuce, chicken, and almonds.

Blend all of the dressing ingredients and lightly toss with the salad.

I find Caesar salad dressing kind of offensive. I've got no problem with the garlic or anchovy paste, but the egg yolks and olive oil are the same base as mayonnaise, and the whole concoction coats the lettuce beyond recognition! That's hardly a salad. My dressing gets its creaminess from nonfat Greek yogurt and a nice tang from the lemon juice and Worcestershire sauce. Better tasting *and* better for you.

Nutrition information: 272 calories, 34g protein, 22g carbs, 8g fat, 9g fiber

Mediterranean Halibut

Olives, lemon, tomatoes, and fish—a classic Mediterranean combination of ingredients. Halibut is seasonally available, so if you can't get it fresh, substitute whatever wild-caught fish is in season.

$1/2$ teaspoon olive oil

$1/4$ cup thinly sliced yellow onion

4 green olives, pitted and halved

1 tablespoon freshly squeezed lemon juice

2 plum tomatoes, chopped, with their juices

4 ounces skinless wild-caught halibut

1 tablespoon chopped fresh parsley

2 cups roasted veggies, warmed before plating

Heat the olive oil in a medium skillet over medium heat. Add the onion and cook for 5 minutes, stirring occasionally.

Reduce the heat to low and stir in the olives, lemon juice, and tomatoes. Cover and simmer for 5 minutes.

Place the fish in the skillet and coat with the sauce. Cover and simmer for 7 to 9 minutes, or until the fish is just cooked through.

Sprinkle with parsley and serve with roasted veggies.

> Roasting vegetables is so easy—plus you can do a huge batch over a weekend and then heat them up again for various recipes all week long. All you need to do is cut your vegetables into pieces about the same size (or, in the case of cauliflower, break it into like-sized florets), toss them in a bowl with some olive oil spray and some minced herbs, and then spread them out in a single layer in a roasting pan or a rimmed baking sheet and cook them at high temperature—450°F will do it—for as long as it takes the vegetable to brown and soften (15 to 30 minutes, depending on the veg).

Nutrition information: 295 calories, 28g protein, 28g carbs, 10g fat, 7g fiber

Dressy Lettuce Wraps

The key to memorable and satisfying lettuce wraps is the dressing. Play around with different herbs and acids (like vinegars or citruses) to find what you like best. Also, have fun with your vegetable toppings—zucchini and cabbage shred easily, but you could also shred carrots or dice tomatoes, cucumbers, or red onion.

WRAP:

Olive oil spray

4 ounces ground white turkey

$1/2$ teaspoon freshly grated ginger

1 garlic clove, crushed

Pinch of freshly ground black pepper

$1/3$ cup shredded zucchini

$1/2$ cup shredded cabbage

2 or 3 big lettuce leaves

DRESSING:

1 teaspoon chopped fresh mint

1 tablespoon freshly squeezed orange juice

$1/2$ teaspoon agave

1 teaspoon rice wine vinegar

Coat a medium skillet with olive oil spray and heat over medium-high heat. Add the turkey, ginger, garlic, and pepper. Cook for 5 minutes, stirring occasionally and breaking the turkey into crumbles. Spoon the turkey onto a paper towel and allow to cool.

Spoon the zucchini and cabbage into the lettuce leaves, then top with the turkey.

Mix the dressing ingredients together and drizzle over the top.

Nutrition information: 205 calories, 24g protein, 10g carbs, 8g fat, 4g fiber

Baked Squash

Baking in a single dish is the most painless preparation possible. Butternut squash, like its other gourd family members, has incredible benefits and, considering its nutritional value, can fill you up without packing on the pounds.

Olive oil spray

1/2 cup 1/2-inch cubes peeled butternut squash

1 cup chopped fresh spinach or kale

1/2 cup plain 2% fat Greek yogurt

2 large egg whites

1 garlic clove, crushed

1/4 teaspoon grated lemon zest

1/2 cup cooked spaghetti squash (see page 84)

3 ounces roasted boneless, skinless chicken breast, cut into cubes

1 tablespoon feta cheese, crumbled

1 1/2 teaspoons chopped fresh mint

> Notice we're using 2% fat Greek yogurt instead of nonfat this time—this is where you're getting the needed, healthy fat for the meal.

Preheat the oven to 375°F. Coat a small baking dish with olive oil spray.

Steam the butternut squash and spinach or kale for 1 minute, then run under cold water.

In a medium bowl, mix the yogurt, egg whites, garlic, and lemon zest. Fold in the spinach or kale, butternut and spaghetti squashes, and chicken.

Pour the mixture into the prepared baking dish. Top with the feta.

Bake for 15 to 20 minutes, until bubbly around the edges. Before serving, stir in the mint.

Nutrition information: 312 calories, 39g protein, 22g carbs, 8g fat, 5g fiber

Halibut with Radish-Leaf Pesto

You know that fish is my favorite protein and halibut is one of my all-time favorites. But this recipe would work with cod or haddock or any firm white fish.

HALIBUT:

1/2 teaspoon olive oil

5 asparagus spears, cut into 1-inch pieces

1 plum tomato, chopped

5 kalamata olives, pitted and halved

1 teaspoon freshly squeezed lemon juice

1 tablespoon chopped fresh parsley

Dash of freshly ground black pepper

4 ounces skinless wild-caught halibut

RADISH-LEAF PESTO:

1/3 cup radish leaves, washed and dried

1 tablespoon freshly squeezed lemon juice

1 1/2 teaspoons grated parmesan cheese

1/4 garlic clove

1 to 2 tablespoons low-sodium chicken or vegetable broth (water will also do)

Preheat the oven to 375°F. Place a piece of foil on a rimmed baking sheet and lightly coat with the olive oil.

Toss together the asparagus, tomato, olives, lemon juice, parsley, and pepper.

Spread the asparagus mixture on the foil.

Top with the halibut and bake for 15 to 20 minutes, or until the fish is flaky and cooked through.

Meanwhile, place the pesto ingredients in the bowl of a food processor or blender and blend until smooth.

Plate the fish and vegetables and top the halibut with pesto.

Nutrition information: 230 calories, 27g protein, 10g carbs, 10g fat, 4g fiber

Until recently, I used to disregard the leaves of a lot of root vegetables. Now, I try to utilize as much of the produce as possible, from root to leaf. Radish leaves are very tasty and can be cooked or made into pesto, a nice change from common ingredients like basil, parsley, and arugula. Just be sure to rinse the leaves before you make the pesto.

Charred Brussels Sprouts with Herby Turkey

If you have an aversion to Brussels sprouts, this dish will help you get over it! The sprouts aren't boiled or steamed (which leaves them limp and cabbagey) but are roasted into a decadent, potato-like crispness.

4 ounces boneless, skinless turkey
    (or chicken) breast

$1/2$ teaspoon grated lemon zest

$1/2$ teaspoon chopped fresh sage

$1/2$ teaspoon chopped fresh rosemary

$1/2$ teaspoon chopped fresh thyme

1 teaspoon olive oil

Olive oil spray

10 Brussels sprouts, halved

5 asparagus spears, each cut into 4 pieces

> Boneless, skinless chicken breast substitutes seamlessly for the turkey breast in this recipe.

Preheat the oven to 400°F.

Place the turkey in a zip-top bag and add the lemon zest, chopped herbs, and olive oil. Massage the seasoning into the poultry and refrigerate for 10 to 15 minutes.

Transfer the turkey to a small baking dish.

Spray a rimmed baking sheet with olive oil spray. Place the Brussels sprouts on the sheet in a single layer and coat with more spray.

Place the turkey and Brussels sprouts side by side in the oven and bake for 15 minutes.

Remove the turkey and Brussels sprouts from the oven.

Add the asparagus to the Brussels sprouts and toss carefully. Return to the oven to bake for an additional 5 minutes while the turkey is resting.

Nutrition information: 249 calories, 30g protein, 21g carbs, 8g fat, 9g fiber

Blackened Mahi Mahi with Fennel Slaw

"Blackened" doesn't mean burnt; it means you'll give the fish a crisp exterior—the result of searing on high heat with a coating of a dried herb rub. And it means delicious!

1 teaspoon herb rub (below)

4 ounces mahi mahi

1 teaspoon olive oil

1/3 cup finely minced fennel bulb

1 tablespoon chopped fennel fronds

1/2 cup shredded zucchini

1/2 teaspoon grated orange zest

1 teaspoon freshly squeezed orange juice

2 cups mixed salad greens

HERB RUB:

This will make more than you need for this one recipe, but you can store it in a zip-top bag and use it another time on other firm fish or even chicken.

Fennel is a hugely underused vegetable. Maybe that's because it looks a little odd and many people aren't sure what part of it to use! In this recipe, you'll use both the bulb and the wispy fronds at the top. Pull the fronds off the long, celery-like stalk and set aside. Cut the stalk off the bulb and then cut the bulb in half to get at the hard core. Cut out that hard center and you'll be left with concave bulb halves, which can then be sliced thinly and minced to make the slaw.

4 teaspoons dried leaf thyme

2 teaspoons onion powder

2 teaspoons garlic powder

2 teaspoons black pepper

1 teaspoon cayenne pepper, or to your taste

1 teaspoon dried leaf oregano

3/4 teaspoon ground cumin

Heat the oven to 400°F.

In a small bowl, combine the herb rub ingredients and pat 1 teaspoon of the seasoning onto both sides of the fillet. Heat an ovenproof skillet over medium-high heat and coat with the olive oil. Sear the fish until blackened, 2 minutes per side, then transfer to the oven and cook for 6 to 8 minutes, until flaky.

In the meantime, mix the minced fennel, fennel fronds, zucchini, orange zest, and orange juice.

Top the fish with the fennel slaw and serve with the mixed greens.

Nutrition information: 209 calories, 29g protein, 11g carbs, 6g fat, 5g fiber

Lemon Garlic Goodness Soup

This lemony, garlicky soup has kale and chicken to boot—it's an all-around good-for-you last meal of the day.

1 teaspoon olive oil

1/4 cup chopped yellow onion

2 garlic cloves, crushed

4 ounces boneless, skinless chicken breast,
   cut into cubes

1 teaspoon herbes de Provence
   (or a combination of dried thyme, rosemary,
   oregano, and basil)

1 bay leaf

2 cups low-sodium chicken broth

2 tablespoons freshly squeezed lemon juice

2 cups chopped kale

> Forget about chicken noodle soup when you're under the weather! Lemon is a great detoxifier and helps flush your system, so combined with garlic, which is packed with antioxidants, and everyone's favorite superfood, kale, you've got yourself a cure.

Heat the olive oil in a soup pot over medium-low heat. Add the onion and garlic; sauté for 5 minutes, stirring occasionally. Add the chicken, herbes de Provence, and bay leaf; raise the heat to medium-high and cook for 5 more minutes.

Pour in the broth and lemon juice. Reduce the heat, cover, and simmer for 20 minutes.

Turn off the heat and remove the bay leaf. Add the kale and stir until slightly wilted.

Nutrition information: 266 calories, 30g protein, 22g carbs, 9g fat, 6g fiber

Beef Stroganoff

My version of this traditionally heavy dish gives you all the flavor you'll remember plus noodles you can eat at night—zucchini noodles!

4 ounces beef top round

Olive oil spray

1 portobello mushroom, cut into $1/2$-inch cubes

$1/4$ cup finely chopped yellow onion

1 garlic clove, crushed

$1/2$ teaspoon paprika

1 cup low-sodium chicken broth

$1/2$ teaspoon Dijon mustard

1 large zucchini

$1/4$ cup plain nonfat Greek yogurt

Pinch of freshly ground black pepper

1 tablespoon chopped fresh parsley

> See the photo that accompanies the recipe for Zucchini Noodles with Avocado Cream Sauce (page 138) for a better sense of how scrumptious these thinly sliced "noodles" can be.

Slice the beef into thin strips, cutting against the grain. Coat a soup pot with olive oil spray and heat over high heat. Add the beef and cook on all sides until browned, 1 to 2 minutes. Remove the beef from the pot and set aside.

Add the mushrooms and cook for 5 minutes, stirring halfway through.

Reduce the heat to medium and coat again with olive oil spray. Add the onion and sauté for 5 minutes, then add the garlic and paprika; cook for 1 minute more while stirring.

Add the broth, mustard, and cooked beef. Bring to a simmer, then reduce the heat to low. Cover the pot and simmer for 20 to 25 minutes to allow the sauce to thicken a bit.

Meanwhile, slice the zucchini very thinly lengthwise, then cut each piece into thirds lengthwise to resemble thick noodles. Steam the "noodles" for 2 to 3 minutes or until they are just cooked through.

Stir the yogurt into the stroganoff; season with the pepper and garnish with the parsley. Serve over the zucchini noodles.

Nutrition information: 284 calories, 35g protein, 19g carbs, 8g fat, 5g fiber

Salmon with Creamy Dill Sauce

Greek yogurt is a Skinny Meals substitute in almost any recipe that calls for sour cream, crème fraiche, or mayonnaise. Combined here with two simple herbs, you'll think you've died and gone to heaven . . . or somewhere in Scandinavia!

$1/2$ teaspoon chopped fresh thyme

1 teaspoon olive oil

1 garlic clove, crushed

$1/2$ cup diced butternut squash

$1/4$ red onion, cut into wedges

Olive oil spray

4 ounces wild-caught salmon

2 teaspoons freshly squeezed lemon juice

CREAM SAUCE:

1 tablespoon finely chopped fresh dill

$1/3$ cup plain nonfat Greek yogurt

$1 1/2$ teaspoons chopped fresh parsley

> Salmon is loaded with health-fortifying omega-3 fatty acids—you want more of those! As with other fish, though, reach for the line-caught or wild salmon to avoid the potential pollutants in some farm-raised fish.

Preheat the oven to 475°F.

Combine the thyme, olive oil, and garlic in a bowl. Add the squash and onion and toss to coat.

Coat a rimmed baking sheet with olive oil spray and arrange the vegetable mixture in a single layer on the pan. Bake for 10 minutes.

Remove the pan from the oven and place the salmon atop the veggies. Sprinkle the lemon juice over the salmon. Cook for 10 more minutes, or until the salmon is cooked through.

Meanwhile, mix together the ingredients for the cream sauce and set aside.

Plate the salmon and vegetables and dollop cream sauce on top of the salmon.

Nutrition information: 242 calories, 29g protein, 17g carbs, 7g fat, 4g fiber

Colorful Stir-Fry

Red cabbage is a great source of potassium, vitamin C, and vitamin A. The vibrant color combination of this stir-fry is a feast to the eyes and your health.

This one converts easily to meatless—just add 1/3 cup tempeh in place of the chicken.

1 teaspoon olive oil

1/4 red onion, cut into thin strips

4 ounces boneless, skinless chicken breast, cut into strips

1/3 cup low-sodium chicken broth

1 cup chopped broccoli

1 cup shredded red cabbage

1 garlic clove, crushed

1/2 teaspoon freshly grated ginger

Crushed red pepper, to your liking

1 tablespoon Bragg Liquid Aminos

1 cup chopped kale

1 tablespoon chopped fresh cilantro

1 1/2 teaspoons chopped fresh basil

Coat a large skillet with olive oil and heat over medium-high heat. Add the onion and cook for 5 minutes, stirring frequently. Add the chicken and cook for 4 minutes more.

Add the broth, broccoli, cabbage, garlic, ginger, red pepper, and Bragg Aminos; cook for 6 minutes, stirring occasionally.

Add the kale, cilantro, and basil. Cook until the kale is wilted.

Nutrition information: 251 calories, 29g protein, 21g carbs, 9g fat, 8g fiber
Meatless option: 247 calories, 17g protein, 26g carbs, 11g fat, 8g fiber

Mighty Meatloaf

Meatloaf is wonderful. It's delicious. However, it's not good when you use meat, whole eggs, and bread crumbs to make it moist. And let's not serve it with heavy mashed potatoes flavored with butter and cream! Here the cauliflower is a fantastic substitute accompaniment.

3 ounces ground white turkey

2 large egg whites

1 tablespoon Dijon mustard

2 tablespoons finely chopped fresh basil

1 tablespoon finely chopped fresh parsley

1 garlic clove, crushed

1 teaspoon tomato paste

$1/4$ teaspoon freshly ground black pepper

Olive oil spray

$1 1/2$ cups chopped cauliflower

$1/2$ cup low-sodium chicken broth

$1/4$ teaspoon dried thyme

2 teaspoons grated parmesan cheese

2 cups chopped fresh spinach

Preheat the oven to 375°F.

In a bowl, hand-mix the turkey, egg whites, mustard, basil, parsley, garlic, tomato paste, and pepper.

Coat 2 muffin cups with olive oil spray and fill with the turkey mixture. Place in the oven and bake for about 20 minutes, or until it's not pink in the middle.

Meanwhile, place the cauliflower in a small pot with the broth and simmer, covered, for 5 to 7 minutes, until it is fork-tender.

Using a slotted spoon, transfer the cauliflower to the bowl of a food processor, reserving the broth. Add the thyme and parmesan and pulse until the cauliflower is smooth, adding broth until the desired consistency is reached; it should be the thickness of mashed potatoes.

In traditional meatloaf, a whole egg (or two) and bread crumbs usually serve to "bind" the ingredients and keep them loaf-like in the cooking process. But you don't need all that to keep the dish in shape—the two egg whites in this recipe will do the trick all on their own.

In a skillet, heat 2 tablespoons of the reserved cooking broth over medium heat. Add the spinach, cover, and cook for 1 to 2 minutes, until the spinach is wilted.

Nutrition information: 239 calories, 31g protein, 15g carbs, 8g fat, 6g fiber

Tangy Shrimp with Coconut "Rice"

This whole meal comes together really quickly. Total cooking time is only about 5 minutes. And you'll use only one skillet!

1 teaspoon olive oil

5 ounces shrimp (about 5 large or 3 jumbo), deveined, shelled, and cleaned

1 tablespoon freshly squeezed lime juice

1 teaspoon agave

1 tablespoon chopped fresh cilantro

1/2 teaspoon chopped jalapeño pepper

2 cups chopped cauliflower

1/4 red bell pepper, thinly sliced

2 tablespoons "lite" coconut milk

1 cup finely chopped fresh spinach

In a small skillet, heat the olive oil over medium heat. Add the shrimp and cook for 3 minutes on each side.

Meanwhile, mix the lime juice, agave, cilantro, and jalapeño. Pour over the shrimp and toss to coat. Cover and cook for 1 more minute. Remove the shrimp and set aside.

To make the coconut "rice," place the cauliflower in the bowl of a food processor and pulse until it becomes ricelike. In the same skillet used for the shrimp, combine the bell pepper and coconut milk. Cover and cook for 2 minutes over medium heat; add the cauliflower "rice" and spinach. Stir and cook for 1 more minute.

Serve with the shrimp on top.

Nutrition information: 289 calories, 34g protein, 22g carbs, 9g fat, 6g fiber

As with several other recipes, you're making "rice" out of cauliflower here. This time, however, you're giving it all kinds of outrageously great flavor with coconut milk. Coconut milk can be very high in calories and fat, so make sure to get the "lite" version to make your meal skinny.

Steak and Warm Spinach Salad

The hot steak will wilt the greens slightly and the juices from the meat will mingle deliciously with the dressing—you'll never want to eat one without the other again! Even still, I advise massaging the sometimes still-tough kale with a spritz of olive oil to tenderize it a bit.

1 tablespoon Bragg Liquid Aminos

1 tablespoon balsamic vinegar

1/2 teaspoon agave

1 garlic clove, crushed

1 teaspoon minced fresh ginger

1 scallion, white and light green parts, thinly sliced

4 ounces lean round steak

Olive oil spray

2 cups chopped fresh spinach

2 cups chopped kale,
    massaged with a spritz of olive oil to tenderize

1/2 red bell pepper, thinly sliced

> Think you can't have a juicy steak and lose weight? Think again! You just need to skip the potatoes part of "meat and potatoes." A lean steak and some power vegetables is a wonderful pairing—lots of protein, lots of fiber. You won't feel hungry again until breakfast!

In a medium bowl, mix the Bragg Aminos, balsamic vinegar, agave, garlic, ginger, and scallion. Add the steak and coat both sides with the marinade. Cover with plastic wrap and marinate overnight.

When ready to cook, heat a skillet (or grill) over medium-high heat. Coat the pan with olive oil spray, add the steak, and cook for at least 3 minutes on each side. Let rest for 5 minutes before cutting.

Mound the spinach, kale, and bell pepper on a plate; slice the steak into thin strips and place on top.

Nutrition information: 294 calories, 31g protein, 26g carbs, 10g fat, 8g fiber

Chicken Romana

This is inspired by a Roman peasant dish that combines table wine and leftover herbs to add flavor and tenderize the meat in an all-day cooking process. Since most of us don't have time for that, and since I've discovered that the table wine isn't necessary, this is my quick, simple, and fresh version.

Olive oil spray

1/4 red onion, thinly sliced

4 ounces boneless, skinless chicken breast, cut into strips

1/2 red bell pepper, cut into thin strips

1/2 yellow bell pepper, cut into thin strips

2 plum tomatoes, quartered

1 garlic clove, crushed

1/2 cup low-sodium chicken broth

2 cups chopped fresh spinach

1 teaspoon chopped fresh oregano

1 tablespoon chopped fresh basil

4 green olives, pitted and quartered

Coat a large skillet with olive oil spray and heat over medium heat. Add the red onion and cook for 5 minutes, stirring occasionally.

Add the chicken and bell peppers; cook for 5 more minutes. Add the tomatoes, garlic, and broth. Reduce the heat to low and bring to a simmer; cook, uncovered, for 10 minutes.

Stir in the spinach, oregano, basil, and green olives. Cook just until the spinach wilts, a minute or two.

Nutrition information: 226 calories, 27g protein, 19g carbs, 9g fat, 5g fiber

Zucchini Noodles with Avocado Cream Sauce

Carb-free noodles—hooray! Thinly sliced zucchini will work in any recipe that calls for pasta. They pair beautifully with any Skinny Rules–approved sauce.

1 large zucchini

4 ounces roasted boneless, skinless chicken breast, warmed before plating

AVOCADO CREAM SAUCE:

$1/4$ avocado

1 cup arugula

$1/4$ cup chopped fresh basil

$1/4$ cup low-sodium vegetable or chicken broth

1 tablespoon freshly squeezed lemon juice

1 teaspoon crushed garlic

2 teaspoons grated parmesan cheese

Slice the zucchini very thinly lengthwise. Then cut each piece into thirds lengthwise to resemble thick noodles. Steam the "noodles" for 2 to 3 minutes or until they are just cooked through.

Meanwhile, blend the avocado, arugula, basil, broth, lemon juice, garlic, and parmesan in a food processor or blender.

Toss the "noodles" with the sauce and the cubed chicken and serve.

If you have a mandoline, use that to slice the zucchini thinly (but watch your fingertips!). If not, use a sharp knife and cut precisely.

Nutrition information: 258 calories, 27g protein, 19g carbs, 11g fat, 8g fiber

Lean Leek Soup

All the flavor and texture and none of the guilt! The cauliflower blended into this soup will make you think you're slurping a creamy sinfulness.

1 teaspoon olive oil

1/3 cup chopped leeks (whites and light green parts)

1 garlic clove, crushed

2 cups low-sodium chicken broth

1 teaspoon fresh thyme leaves

1 bay leaf

1 cup cauliflower florets

4 ounces roasted boneless, skinless chicken breast, cut into cubes

2 cups chopped fresh spinach

Leeks harbor dirt in their folds. To clean them properly, lop off the "hairy" bottom, slice the leek in half lengthwise, then hold the halves together and slice the leek into thin rounds (half rounds, really). Submerge the cut leeks in a bowl of water. Mix them around and let them sit. The dirt will loosen up and fall to the bottom of the bowl in just a few minutes. Scoop the leeks out with your hands or a slotted spoon and give them another rinse in a colander for good measure.

In a soup pot, heat the olive oil over medium heat, then add the leeks and garlic and sauté for 5 minutes, stirring occasionally.

Add the broth, thyme, bay leaf, and cauliflower. Bring to a simmer, then reduce the heat to low and cover. Simmer for 15 minutes.

Remove from the heat and let cool for 15 minutes. Discard the bay leaf.

Transfer the soup to a blender and puree until smooth.

Pour the mixture back into the pot and heat through. Add the chicken and spinach; stir until the spinach is wilted and the chicken is warmed through.

Nutrition information: 226 calories, 28g protein, 14g carbs, 8g fat, 5g fiber

Chicken with Spicy Swiss Chard Salsa Verde

Dark leafy greens aren't just for sautéing! As in this recipe, they can be used as a base for salsas and other sauces. Don't be afraid to experiment. Chard makes this sauce a little reminiscent of the spicy dipping sauces you find in Indian restaurants.

1 cup chopped Swiss chard

1 teaspoon crushed garlic

1 1/2 teaspoons minced jalapeño pepper, ribs and seeds removed

1/8 to 1/4 cup low-sodium chicken broth (depending on desired consistency)

1 tablespoon freshly squeezed lime juice

1 teaspoon olive oil

4 ounces roasted boneless, skinless chicken breast, warmed before plating

2 cups roasted veggies, warmed before plating

In a food processor or blender, combine the Swiss chard, garlic, jalapeño, broth (start with 1/8 cup and add more as needed), lime juice, and olive oil and blend until smooth.

Top the chicken with Swiss chard salsa and serve with roasted veggies.

Nutrition information: 266 calories, 29g protein, 25g carbs, 9g fat, 8g fiber

Chicken, Fennel, and Grapefruit Salad

Fennel has a mild licorice flavor that isn't to everyone's liking. Even if that describes you, try this recipe just once anyway and see if you aren't converted! Slice the fennel very thin and you'll get its crunch without so much of its anise flavor.

1 small bulb of fennel

1 pink grapefruit

1 teaspoon olive oil

1 teaspoon red wine vinegar

2 teaspoons agave

4 ounces roasted boneless,
    skinless chicken breast, shredded

1 cup chopped fresh spinach

1 cup chopped arugula

> See page 127 for tips on how to cut up a fennel bulb. Once you take out the hard heart, or core, of the bulb, you could also slice it by using the slicing disk of a food processor.

Cut the stalks from the top of the fennel bulb. Cut the bulb in half, remove and discard the core, and thinly slice. Tear off the wispy fronds and set aside.

Section the grapefruit by first peeling it, making sure to get rid of the white pith. Working over a bowl (to catch the juice), use a paring knife to cut out the grapefruit segments one by one, setting them aside. When done, squeeze the remaining flesh over the bowl to get the last of the juice.

Mix 1 tablespoon of the grapefruit juice with the olive oil, vinegar, and agave.

Lightly toss the dressing with the fennel, sectioned grapefruit, and chicken.

Serve on a bed of spinach and arugula; garnish with fennel fronds.

Nutrition information: 239 calories, 25g protein, 22g carbs, 8g fat, 4g fiber

Tomato and Garlic Cod with Steamed Veggies

This light fish and vegetable dish is a completely well-balanced meal you can have any night of the week. To vary it, play with different spices or citruses in the sauce.

1 teaspoon olive oil

4 ounces skinless wild-caught cod or sea bass fillet

2 plum tomatoes, diced

1 garlic clove, crushed

1 tablespoon chopped fresh parsley

7 asparagus spears, steamed

2 cups chopped fresh spinach, steamed

1 tablespoon freshly squeezed lemon juice

Preheat the oven to 375°F.

Coat an ovenproof skillet with the olive oil and heat over medium heat. Add the fish and cook for 90 seconds on one side.

Meanwhile, in a small bowl, mix the tomatoes and garlic.

Flip the fish and add the tomato and garlic. Transfer the skillet to the oven and bake for 10 to 12 minutes, or until the fish is flaky and cooked through.

Place the fish on a plate. Stir the parsley into the tomato sauce and pour over the fish.

Serve with asparagus and spinach, drizzled with the lemon juice.

Nutrition information: 224 calories, 31g protein, 13g carbs, 6g fat, 5g fiber

Thai Soup

Don't be intimidated by the number of ingredients in this dish. Once you've chopped or measured everything, the assembly is very quick—and all in one pot!

Olive oil spray

2 scallions, white and light green parts, thinly sliced

1 garlic clove, minced

1 teaspoon freshly grated ginger

1 jalapeño pepper, thinly sliced

4 crimini mushrooms, stemmed and thinly sliced

3 ounces boneless, skinless chicken breast, cut into thin strips

1 cup low-sodium chicken broth

1/4 cup "lite" coconut milk

1 cup chopped broccoli

1/2 cup chopped cabbage

1 large zucchini

1 tablespoon chopped fresh cilantro

1 tablespoon chopped fresh basil

1 or 2 lime wedges

> If you're feeling adventurous, you can also add a little splash of fish sauce, which is a classic ingredient in Thai cuisine. By itself, it's way too daring for my liking, but when you add it to the broth, coconut, basil, and cilantro, it adds a nice background flavor.

Coat a soup pot with olive oil spray and heat over medium-high heat. Add the scallions, garlic, and ginger and sauté for 4 minutes, stirring frequently. Add the jalapeño and mushrooms and cook until softened, about 3 minutes. Add the chicken, broth, and coconut milk. Bring to a boil, then reduce the heat, cover, and simmer for 15 minutes.

Add the broccoli and cabbage and simmer, covered, for another 5 minutes.

Meanwhile, slice the zucchini very thinly lengthwise. Then cut each piece into thirds lengthwise to resemble thick noodles.

Add the "noodles" and cook for another 2 to 3 minutes, or until they are just cooked through.

Top with the cilantro and basil. Serve with lime wedges.

Nutrition information: 243 calories, 25g protein, 22g carbs, 9g fat, 8g fiber

Chimichurri Steak

Chimichurri is an Argentinean sauce similar to pesto. You will often see it with more olive oil than herbs, but to make it skinny, I swapped the base and created a more herbaceous condiment.

Olive oil spray

1 cup sliced bell peppers

1/4 red onion, thinly sliced

3 plum tomatoes, quartered

2 cups chopped fresh spinach

4 ounces lean round steak

CHIMICHURRI SAUCE:

1 tablespoon chopped fresh parsley

1 tablespoon chopped fresh cilantro

1 teaspoon chopped fresh mint

1/2 garlic clove

1 teaspoon freshly squeezed lemon juice

2 tablespoons low-sodium chicken broth

> Chimichurri isn't only for Argentineans—it's popular throughout South America. And chimichurri isn't only for steak—you can use this as a marinade for any protein, as a sauce for lunch pasta, as a topping on eggs, or as a dressing.

Heat a medium skillet over medium-high heat. Coat the skillet with olive oil spray and add the bell peppers and red onion. Cook for 5 minutes, then add the tomatoes and spinach. Heat through, stirring, until the spinach wilts. Remove the vegetables from the pan and set aside.

Place the steak in the hot skillet and cook for at least 3 minutes on each side. Transfer to a cutting board and let rest for 5 minutes before slicing.

Meanwhile, combine the parsley, cilantro, mint, garlic, lemon juice, and broth in a food processor or blender and process until coarsely blended.

Cut the steak into strips and serve on top of the vegetables. Drizzle the chimichurri sauce over the steak.

Nutrition information: 262 calories, 29g protein, 20g carbs, 10g fat, 5g fiber

Hearty Turkey Kale Soup

You'll notice I don't use carrots here—they have a lot of sugar and I steer clear of them at night—but you could add celery along with the onion, garlic, and bay leaf, and if you want more flavor, add more spices.

1 teaspoon olive oil

1/4 cup chopped yellow onion

1 garlic clove, crushed

1 bay leaf

1/2 teaspoon dried thyme

3 ounces ground turkey

2 cups low-sodium chicken broth

2 cups chopped kale

2 teaspoons grated parmesan cheese

> You can always replace dry herbs with fresh ones, but keep in mind that dry herbs pack more of a flavor punch than fresh. As a general rule, you should double the amount of fresh herbs if a recipe calls for a dried herb. For instance, if a recipe calls for 1 teaspoon of dried thyme, use 2 teaspoons of fresh.

Coat a soup pot with the olive oil and heat over medium heat. Add the onion, garlic, and bay leaf. Sauté for 5 minutes, stirring frequently. Add the thyme and turkey and cook for 3 minutes, stirring to break the turkey into crumbles. Add the broth and bring to a boil; then cover, reduce the heat, and simmer for 10 minutes.

Remove the bay leaf. Add the kale and simmer until just wilted, stirring all along.

Serve with a sprinkling of parmesan.

Nutrition information: 264 calories, 28g protein, 20g carbs, 9g fat, 6g fiber

Creole Shrimp

Creole food is traditionally very heavy. It uses a lot of butter, a lot of cream, and a lot of fatty sausage and meats. But once you understand the Creole spice combos, you can eliminate the fats yet keep all the taste.

1 teaspoon olive oil

1/4 cup chopped onion

1 garlic clove, minced

1/2 cup chopped red bell pepper

1 celery stalk, finely chopped

2 plum tomatoes

A few drops of Tabasco sauce, or to taste

Pinch of freshly ground black pepper

1/2 teaspoon dried thyme

4 ounces shrimp, peeled and deveined

2 cups chopped Swiss chard

1 tablespoon chopped fresh parsley

1 lemon, cut into quarters

Coat a large skillet with the olive oil and heat over medium heat. Add the onion, garlic, bell pepper, and celery and sauté until tender.

Add the tomatoes, Tabasco, pepper, and thyme. Simmer over low heat, stirring occasionally, for 10 minutes.

Add the shrimp and cook for 5 minutes, flipping halfway through.

Add the Swiss chard and cook until wilted.

Sprinkle with the parsley and serve with the lemon wedges.

Nutrition information: 300 calories, 32g protein, 32g carbs, 8g fat, 10g fiber

Almond-Crusted Chicken with Balsamic Green Beans

Lightly coating the chicken with the egg and almond meal batter will give you the mock fried texture you're probably craving. The balsamic vinegar on the green beans adds a little sweetness, too.

1 tablespoon almond meal

1 tablespoon grated parmesan cheese

1 tablespoon unsweetened almond milk

1 large egg white

1 tablespoon Dijon mustard

4 ounces boneless, skinless chicken breast

Olive oil spray

1 cup green beans

1 teaspoon balsamic vinegar

> Almond meal is really just ground-up almonds, but I recommend buying the meal instead of trying to grind your own almonds at home!

Preheat the oven to 375°F.

On a plate, mix the almond meal and parmesan.

In a shallow bowl, beat the almond milk, egg white, and mustard.

Dip the chicken in the egg mixture, then lightly coat with half of the almond-cheese mixture. Repeat.

Coat an ovenproof skillet with olive oil spray. Heat over medium-high heat. Add the chicken and cook for 3 minutes on each side, then transfer the skillet to the oven. Bake for 12 to 15 minutes, until no longer pink in the center.

Meanwhile, steam the green beans until just tender (check after 2 minutes to be sure you don't overcook) and toss with the vinegar; serve alongside the chicken.

Nutrition information: 224 calories, 31g protein, 10g carbs, 8g fat, 5g fiber

French Halibut with Green Beans

You don't need cream or butter to feel like you've landed in Paris! Dijon mustard and tarragon are a classic French flavor combination, perked up here with just a little orange juice. *C'est magnifique!*

4 ounces skinless wild-caught halibut

1 teaspoon olive oil

1 tablespoon grated parmesan cheese

Olive oil spray

1 1/2 cups sliced green beans

2 tablespoons freshly squeezed orange juice

1 teaspoon Dijon mustard

1 teaspoon chopped fresh tarragon

1 tablespoon water

2 cups mixed salad greens

Freshly squeezed lemon juice to taste

Preheat the oven to 375°F.

Coat the halibut with the olive oil and parmesan.

Place a piece of foil (about 8 inches long) on a baking sheet. Lightly coat with olive oil spray. Place the halibut on the foil and bake for 10 to 15 minutes, or until flaky and cooked through.

Meanwhile, steam the green beans until just tender.

Mix together the orange juice, mustard, tarragon, and water. Spoon on top of the halibut.

Serve with the green beans and mixed greens dressed with fresh lemon juice.

Nutrition information: 260 calories, 30g protein, 17g carbs, 10g fat, 8g fiber

Roasted Tomato and Basil Hummus

Hummus is versatile—play with the flavors! If you want to try a spicy hummus, add cilantro and jalapeño. A less spicy but no less tasty option is to use roasted red peppers instead.

My Signature No-Oil Hummus (page 67)

1/3 cup roasted tomatoes (see sidebar)

1/4 cup chopped fresh basil

Prepare the hummus. Blend the tomatoes and basil until smooth, then stir them into the prepared hummus.

Serve with sliced peppers, celery, Persian cucumbers, broccoli . . .

Nutrition information: 100 calories, 4g protein, 20g carbs, 1g fat, 8g fiber

Roasting tomatoes is easy. You can make them ahead and store: Just core 3 ripe tomatoes and toss them, whole, with 2 whole cloves of garlic and some olive oil spray. Place the tomatoes and garlic on a rimmed baking sheet, cover with foil, and roast at 450°F for about an hour. After you've let them cool a bit, you'll be able to squeeze the roasted garlic from the skin and combine it with the tomatoes and any fresh herbs you have on hand. This will yield more than the 1/3 cup of roasted tomatoes you need here, but you can use the leftover tomatoes on an open-faced sandwich for lunch tomorrow or over some poached chicken tomorrow night.

Spiced Almonds

There's nothing wrong with plain almonds as a snack, but why not go a tad more gourmet to mix things up? This recipe would also work with walnuts or pistachios.

1 cup raw almonds

Olive oil spray

1 tablespoon chopped fresh rosemary leaves

Preheat the oven to 300°F.

Coat the almonds with olive oil spray and mix with the rosemary in a small baking dish.

Bake, stirring occasionally, until lightly toasted, 10 to 15 minutes. Let cool.

> You can make these almonds with other spice combinations, too. Instead of rosemary, try 1 teaspoon chili powder for a spicier snack. Or, for a more Mediterranean taste, lightly toss the almonds with a splash of balsamic vinegar and a pinch of herbes de Provence.

Serves 6

Nutrition information: 136 calories, 5g protein, 5g carbs, 12g fat, 3g fiber

Mango Caprese

Caprese is a tomato-based Italian bread topper (bruschetta). You can play around with this and use other fruits, including peaches, pineapple, and papaya. Use the turkey and the cucumber slices as little platforms for the caprese "salsa" and avoid the carbs of crackers or bread.

$1/2$ cup chopped mango

1 tablespoon chopped fresh basil

1 tablespoon finely minced red onion

1 teaspoon balsamic vinegar

6 to 8 cucumber slices

3 slices of low-sodium deli turkey, cut or folded into cucumber-round size

Lightly toss the mango, basil, onion, and vinegar.

Serve the "salsa" on top of the cucumber slices and turkey.

Nutrition information: 104 calories, 8g protein, 17g carbs, 1g fat, 2g fiber

Smashed Pea "Guac"

The green goodness of peas and mint gets a creamy, guacamole-like texture from the Greek yogurt and a little fresh zing from lime juice and agave—happy snacking indeed!

3/4 cup frozen green peas, thawed

1 teaspoon chopped fresh mint

1/4 cup plain nonfat Greek yogurt

2 teaspoons freshly squeezed lime juice

1/2 teaspoon agave

> Peas are high in fiber, vitamin A, and iron, so feel free to put them in soups or on your salads as well.

Place all of the ingredients in the bowl of a food processor and pulse until well combined but still a little chunky.

Serve with Persian cucumber, raw zucchini, jicama, or cauliflower (or a combo).

Nutrition information: 134 calories, .5g fat, 22g carbs, 11g protein, 6g fiber

Greek Yogurt with Stone Fruit or Berries

Hemp seed is a nutritional powerhouse—a complete protein that provides all essential amino acids. It will add a mild nutty flavor to your snack. Pour the yogurt and fruit mixture into Popsicle forms or even into ice trays and freeze them overnight—you'll have yourself a cool treat!

1 6-ounce container of plain nonfat Greek yogurt

$1/2$ cup chopped plums, peaches, or nectarines or $1/2$ cup mixed berries

1 teaspoon agave

1 teaspoon hemp seed

Top the yogurt with the fruit, a drizzle of agave, and a sprinkling of hemp seeds.

Nutrition information: 148 calories, 20g protein, 15g carbs, 2g fat, 3g fiber

Flavored yogurt tends to be packed with an extraordinary amount of sugar, and you're supposed to be severing your ties to the sweet stuff, remember (Rule 10)? When you flavor plain yogurt with chopped or smashed fresh fruit, you'll get a natural, guilt-free sweet treat and some fiber too!

Jicama Slaw

Jicama is a root vegetable that looks like a big, oddly shaped potato, but nutritionally it's nothing like it! Jicama is extremely low in calories, full of fiber and vitamins, and because it is sturdy like a carrot, it's perfect for dipping in hummus. In this slaw, that texture adds a good crunch to every bite.

$1/2$ cup shredded jicama

$1/2$ apple, cut into matchsticks

$1/3$ cup shredded red cabbage

1 tablespoon freshly squeezed lime juice

1 teaspoon agave

Toss all the ingredients together.

Nutrition information: 95 calories, 1g protein, 23g carbs, 0g fat, 7g fiber

Espresso Smoothie

Got coffee left over in the pot you brewed this morning? Here's what you do with it! You don't have to add protein powder if you don't have it on hand, but it will make this snack-time treat more filling and satisfying.

1 small frozen banana

1 teaspoon ground espresso beans (or $1/2$ cup cold leftover black coffee)

$1/2$ cup unsweetened vanilla almond milk

1 cup ice

1 scoop of either chocolate or vanilla protein powder (optional)

Combine all of the ingredients in a blender and enjoy!

Nutrition information: 105 calories, 2g protein, 24g carbs, 2g fat, 3g fiber
With 1 scoop of protein powder: 205 calories, 17g protein, 30g carbs, 3g fat, 6g fiber

In *Jumpstart to Skinny* I recommend having an espresso—or two or three!—a day because caffeine revs your metabolism and has been shown to raise performance levels during exercise. But not for nothing, it also just tastes good! Blend it into this energy-packed snack for an extra boost midmorning or mid-afternoon. You can also throw in a handful of raspberries or strawberries to meet Rule 6 for the day.

Apple with Almond Butter

You hardly need a recipe for these three snack ideas, but sometimes it's good to state the obvious—I don't want any of you complaining that you couldn't figure out what to eat at snack time!

An apple with some almond butter makes a nutritious and filling daily snack. Plus it fulfills Rule 6!

1 apple

1 tablespoon unsweetened almond butter

Cut the apple into wedges and smear with the almond butter.

Nutrition information: 193 calories, 3g protein, 29g carbs, 9g fat, 6g fiber

PART III

SKINNY TOOLS: SHOP, PREPARE, EAT!

'll say it again: You won't break any Skinny Rules if you pick one meal from each recipe category a day. But if you don't want to leave anything to chance (like, say, not being able to decide which fantastically delicious recipe you want to make . . . and so you get fattening takeout instead!), rely on this section—it makes those decisions for you. I've laid out a month's worth of menus here, and have also included handy shopping lists, organized by grocery store sections so you can get in and out quickly. If you've done the pantry shopping well, the items in the weekly "miscellaneous" category may already be in your kitchen. If that's the case, you can interpret the "miscellaneous" category to mean "make sure you've still got this on hand!"

All that said, four weeks' worth of menus—what to eat for breakfast, lunch, dinner, and snacks—doesn't even use all of the recipes in this book. There are twelve recipes (six lunches and six dinners) that I haven't put into this monthlong rotation. Feel free to substitute any of the "leftover" lunch and dinner options for listed recipes that don't really appeal to you. Mix, match, repeat recipes you adore. Shop, chop, and enjoy—and start to lose weight!

WEEK 1

See page 21 for the do-ahead master list of everything you should have in your pantry.

WEEK 1 SHOPPING LISTS

See page 21 for the do-ahead master list of everything you should have in your pantry. As long as you have those staples, you'll only have to shop for the following lists of fresh items (organized by supermarket categories to make your trip to the store quick and purposeful).

Produce Section Shopping List

Fruit

1 peach

1 pear

7 apples

1 mango

1 kiwi

3 or 4 pints fresh berries (raspberries, blueberries, strawberries)

2 avocados

3 limes

4 lemons

1 orange

Vegetables

You may have some leftover vegetables, but as you know, that's okay, because you can and should add these veggies to any meal you make—you just can't have too many greens!

1 pint cherry tomatoes

4 plum tomatoes

1 bag of arugula

7 to 10 Persian cucumbers

1 bag of spinach

1 bag/container of mixed salad greens

1 bag or bunch of kale

1 jalapeño pepper

3 red bell peppers

1 large spaghetti squash

2 large zucchini

1 yellow squash

1 head of broccoli (or 1 bag of florets)

2 heads of cauliflower (or 2 bags of florets)

3 large carrots

1 head of red or green cabbage

1 jicama

Fresh Herbs

You can't have too many fresh herbs on hand; I encourage you to get full bunches of parsley, cilantro, and basil. You can probably get away with smaller quantities of the other herbs here, but if you like a specific taste, get more and add it to any of your favorite week 1 recipes.

Basil

Thyme

Dill

Chives

Parsley

Mint

Cilantro

Eggs and Dairy Section Shopping list

4 or 5 single-serving containers of plain nonfat Greek yogurt

1 small container of plain 2% fat Greek yogurt

4 single-serving containers of low-fat cottage cheese

1 small bag of low-fat shredded mozzarella cheese

1 quart unsweetened almond milk

2 dozen omega-3 eggs

Meat/Seafood Section Shopping List

For most of these items you'll have to stop by the meat or seafood counter and ask for these small portions; packaged meats and seafood tend to be family-sized.

6 boneless, skinless chicken breasts

4 ounces lean ground turkey

4 ounces turkey cutlets

4 ounces wild salmon

4 ounces low-sodium deli turkey

3 ounces lean ground beef

5 ounces raw shrimp

Miscellaneous Items Shopping List

You can shop for more than a week's worth of the following items; they will keep in the refrigerator, which will make the next week's shopping that much easier. You may have shopped for these things when restocking your pantry, but it doesn't hurt to be sure you have them on hand.

Kalamata olives (fresh or canned, pitted)

Oil-packed sun-dried tomatoes

Ezekiel bread and Ezekiel tortillas (found in the freezer section)

Walnuts, cashews, or pine nuts (for my pesto recipe, which you can make up to five
    days ahead—just keep it refrigerated)

Do yourself the following favors before your busy week begins:

- Hard-boil half a dozen eggs.
- Make a batch of the Greek yogurt waffles and freeze all but one serving. If you find you're in a rush later this week (or next) and just can't make the day's breakfast recipe, you can toast a waffle and have it on the go with some berries.
- Make a couple of batches of Spiced Almonds (page 158) for satisfying snacks. Store in zip-top bags.
- Whip up a batch of My Signature No-Oil Hummus (page 67)—it's great as is, but you might also want to add in roasted tomatoes and basil if you're following the menus for this week. Store in the fridge.
- Oven-roast a couple of tomatoes (for the hummus) (see sidebar on page 156) and store in the fridge.
- Oven-roast two boneless, skinless chicken breasts so that you have the precooked chicken on hand for this week's menu. Store the roasted chicken in the fridge.

WEEK 1 MENUS

DAY 1

Breakfast:

H$_2$Ox2
Coffee or green tea
Avocado Toast (page 30)

Morning Snack:

H$_2$Ox2
Espresso Smoothie (page 164) with berries

Lunch:

H_2Ox2
Coffee, tea, or seltzer water
Terrific Tuna Salad (page 71)

Afternoon Snack:

H_2Ox2
Roasted Tomato and Basil Hummus (page 156)

Dinner:

H_2Ox2
Seltzer water
Pan-Seared Salmon with Zucchini and Yellow Squash (page 108)

DAY 2

Breakfast:

H_2Ox2
Coffee or green tea
Greek Yogurt Waffle (page 38) and an apple

Morning Snack:

H_2Ox2
Spiced Almonds (page 158)

Lunch:

H_2Ox2
Coffee, tea, or seltzer water
"Makes Me Happy" Egg Salad Sandwich (page 66)

Afternoon Snack:

H_2Ox2

Balsamic Cottage Cheese (page 166) with peppers or berries

Dinner:

H_2Ox2

Seltzer water

Spaghetti Squash Casserole (page 110)

DAY 3

Breakfast:

H_2Ox2

Coffee or green tea

Eggs Florentine (page 42)

Morning Snack:

H_2Ox2

Roasted Tomato and Basil Hummus (page 156)

Lunch:

H_2Ox2

Coffee, tea, or seltzer water

Greek Burger with Sun-Dried Tomato "Aioli" (page 73)

Afternoon Snack:

H_2Ox2

Apple with Almond Butter (page 165) and a side of berries

Dinner:

H_2Ox2
Seltzer water
Chinese Chicken Salad (page 116)

DAY 4

Breakfast:

H_2Ox2
Coffee or green tea
Baked Quinoatmeal (page 40)

Morning Snack:

H_2Ox2
Apple with Almond Butter (page 165)

Lunch:

H_2Ox2
Coffee, tea, or seltzer water
Peach Salad with Chicken (page 60)

Afternoon Snack:

H_2Ox2
Jicama Slaw (page 163)

Dinner:

H_2Ox2
Seltzer water
Enchilada Soup (page 115)

Breakfast:

H$_2$Ox2

Coffee or green tea

Red Egg Skillet (page 50) and an apple

Morning Snack:

H$_2$Ox2

Mango Caprese (page 159)

Lunch:

H$_2$Ox2

Coffee, tea, or seltzer water

Saucy Spring Roll (page 62)

Afternoon Snack:

H$_2$Ox2

Greek Yogurt with Strawberries (page 162)

Dinner:

H$_2$Ox2

Seltzer water

Mighty Meatloaf (page 133)

DAY 6—MEATLESS

Breakfast:

H$_2$Ox2

Coffee or green tea

Spicy Green Shake (page 33)

Morning Snack:

H$_2$Ox2
Spiced Almonds (page 158)

Lunch:

H$_2$Ox2
Coffee, tea, or seltzer water
Pesto Quesadilla (made with beans) (page 65)

Afternoon Snack:

H$_2$Ox2
Apple with Almond Butter (page 165)

Dinner:

H$_2$Ox2
Seltzer water
Chicken Curry over Cauliflower "Rice" (substitute tempeh for chicken)
    (page 111)

DAY 7

Breakfast:

H$_2$Ox2
Coffee or green tea
Eggs Florentine (page 42)

Morning Snack:

H$_2$Ox2
Espresso Smoothie (page 164) with a side of berries

Lunch:

H_2Ox2

Coffee, tea, or seltzer water

Spaghetti Squash Pad Thai (page 84)

Afternoon Snack:

H_2Ox2

Apple with Almond Butter (page 165)

Dinner:

H_2Ox2

Seltzer water

Tangy Shrimp with Coconut "Rice" (page 134)

WEEK 2

Produce Section Shopping List

Fruit

7 apples

3 or 4 pints berries (raspberries, blueberries, strawberries)

1 peach

1 kiwi

1 mango

1 banana

2 figs

4 lemons

3 limes

1 avocado

Vegetables

2 red bell peppers

1 green bell pepper

1 jalapeño pepper

7 to 10 Persian cucumbers

1 small bunch of asparagus

10 to 12 Brussels sprouts

2 zucchini

1 small head of broccoli (or 1 bag of florets)

1 bag of spinach

1 bag/container of mixed salad greens

1 bag/container of arugula

1 bunch of kale

1 pint cherry tomatoes

8 plum tomatoes

5 celery stalks

1/2 butternut squash (if not sold in halves, buy the precut squash and store what you
    don't use this week in an airtight container for next week)

1 head of red or green cabbage

1 jicama

1 bunch of radishes with leaves still on

2 packages of mixed wild mushrooms

1 portobello mushroom

Fresh Herbs

As I said for week 1, you can't have too many fresh herbs on hand. If you can buy
small quantities of most of these herbs, you won't waste them. If you have found you
love one particular fresh herb, get a big bunch of that one (or ones) and add it to
whatever you like this week.

Basil

Oregano

Parsley

Rosemary

Thyme

Dill

Tarragon

Chives

Cilantro

Mint

Eggs and Dairy Section Shopping List

5 or 6 single-serving containers of plain nonfat Greek yogurt

4 small containers of low-fat cottage cheese

1 small bag of low-fat shredded mozzarella cheese

2 dozen omega-3 eggs

Meat/Seafood Section Shopping List

8 boneless, skinless chicken breasts

3 ounces lean ground turkey

4 ounces wild salmon

4 ounces wild halibut

4 ounces sliced low-sodium deli turkey

4 ounces lean beef round

Miscellaneous Items Shopping List

Kalamata olives (fresh or canned, pitted)

1 whole-grain bun (you can buy one at a time in the bakery section of most grocery
stores)

Walnuts, cashews, or pine nuts

DO-AHEAD DETAILS

- Hard-boil 6 eggs.
- Make up a batch of My Signature No-Oil Hummus (page 67).
- Oven-roast 2 plum tomatoes (see sidebar on page 156) and keep them in the fridge to add to the hummus later this week.
- Oven-roast 5 boneless, skinless chicken breasts and store in a sealed container in the refrigerator.
- Put 1 banana in the freezer!

DAY 1

Breakfast:

H_2Ox2
Coffee or green tea
Apple Pie Shake (page 32)

Morning Snack:

H_2Ox2
Greek Yogurt with Berries (page 162)

Lunch:

H_2Ox2
Coffee, tea, or seltzer water
Lentil Salad with Herb Dressing (page 92)

Afternoon Snack:

H_2Ox2
Roasted Tomato and Basil Hummus (page 156)

Dinner:

H_2Ox2
Seltzer water
Poached Chicken with Lemon, Capers, and Parsley Gremolata (page 119)

Breakfast:

H$_2$Ox2
Coffee or green tea
Overloaded Toast (page 37)

Morning Snack:

H$_2$Ox2
Balsamic Cottage Cheese (page 166) with peppers or berries

Lunch:

H$_2$Ox2
Coffee, tea, or seltzer water
"Makes Me Happy" Egg Salad Sandwich (page 66)

Afternoon Snack:

H$_2$Ox2
Apple with Almond Butter (page 165) and a side of berries

Dinner:

H$_2$Ox2
Seltzer water
Salmon with Creamy Dill Sauce (page 131)

Breakfast:

H$_2$Ox2
Coffee or green tea
Breakfast Tacos (page 45)

Morning Snack:

H_2Ox2

Smashed Pea "Guac" (page 161)

Lunch:

H_2Ox2

Coffee, tea, or seltzer water

Turkey and Fig Jam Panini (page 88)

Afternoon Snack:

H_2Ox2

Apple with Almond Butter (page 165) and a side of berries

Dinner:

H_2Ox2

Seltzer water

Zucchini Noodles with Avocado Cream Sauce (page 139)

DAY 4

Breakfast:

H_2Ox2

Coffee or green tea

Peachy Keen Smoothie (page 35)

Morning Snack:

H_2Ox2

Mango Caprese (page 159)

Lunch:

H$_2$Ox2

Coffee, tea, or seltzer water

Turkey Clean Joes (page 77)

Afternoon Snack:

H$_2$Ox2

Apple with Almond Butter (page 165) and a side of berries

Dinner:

H$_2$Ox2

Seltzer water

Halibut with Radish-Leaf Pesto (page 124)

DAY 5

Breakfast:

H$_2$Ox2

Coffee or green tea

Wild Mushroom Omelet (page 49)

Morning Snack:

H$_2$Ox2

Apple with Almond Butter (page 165) and a side of berries

Lunch:

H$_2$Ox2

Coffee, tea, or seltzer water

Cajun Chicken Sandwich (page 74)

Afternoon Snack:

H_2Ox2
Espresso Smoothie (page 164) with berries

Dinner:

H_2Ox2
Seltzer water
Beef Stroganoff (page 130)

DAY 6—MEATLESS

Breakfast:

H_2Ox2
Coffee or green tea
Leaner Loco Moco (page 36)

Morning Snack:

H_2Ox2
Apple with Almond Butter (page 165) and a side of berries

Lunch:

H_2Ox2
Coffee, tea, or seltzer water
Perfect Pasta Salad (made with tempeh or beans) (page 63)

Afternoon Snack:

H_2Ox2
Jicama Slaw (page 163)

Dinner:

H_2Ox2

Seltzer water

Colorful Stir-Fry (made with beans) (page 132)

Breakfast:

H_2Ox2

Coffee or green tea

Spicy Green Shake (page 33)

Morning Snack:

H_2Ox2

Spiced Almonds (page 158) and an apple

Lunch:

H_2Ox2

Coffee, tea, or seltzer water

Pesto Quesadilla (page 65)

Afternoon Snack:

H_2Ox2

Balsamic Cottage Cheese (page 166) with mixed berries

Dinner:

H_2Ox2

Seltzer water

Brussels Sprout Chicken Caesar Salad (page 120)

WEEK 3

Produce Section Shopping List

Fruit

7 apples

3 or 4 pints fresh berries (make sure to get blueberries this week)

4 lemons

2 limes

2 bananas

2 oranges

1 avocado

Vegetables

1 small bunch of asparagus

3 zucchini

3 red bell peppers

1 yellow bell pepper

1 jalapeño pepper

9 plum tomatoes

1 pint cherry tomatoes

3 sweet potatoes

1 eggplant

1 bunch of collard greens

1 bunch of kale

1 fennel bulb (with fronds)

1 bag of spinach

1 bag/container of mixed salad greens

1 bunch/bag of arugula

7 to 10 Persian cucumbers

1 bunch of radishes (you won't need the leaves this week, but they are a tasty and
   nutritious green so there's no harm in buying the radishes this way)

1 large carrot

1 small head of cauliflower (or 1 bag of florets)

1 small head of broccoli (or 1 bag of florets)

1 small head of red cabbage

1 small handful of green beans

Fresh Herbs

Dill

Basil

Mint

Cilantro

Rosemary

Thyme

Tarragon

Eggs and Dairy Section Shopping List

5 single-serving containers of plain nonfat Greek yogurt

1 single-serving container of plain 2% fat Greek yogurt

2 to 4 single-serving containers of low-fat cottage cheese

Small container of feta cheese

1 pint unsweetened almond milk

2 dozen omega-3 eggs

Meat/Seafood Section Shopping List

4 ounces pork loin

8 boneless, skinless chicken breasts

8 ounces sliced low-sodium deli turkey

4 ounces wild halibut

4 ounces mahi mahi

3 ounces lean ground beef

Miscellaneous Items Shopping List

Small jar of unsweetened applesauce
Unsalted pumpkin seeds
1 package of tempeh

DO-AHEAD DETAILS

- Hard-boil 6 eggs.
- Make 2 batches of Spiced Almonds (page 158) and store in small plastic bags.
- Make 2 batches of Blueberry Muffins (page 51) and store in an airtight plastic bag.
- Oven-roast 5 boneless, skinless chicken breasts and store in a covered container in the fridge.
- Cook 1 sweet potato. Wrap in foil and refrigerate.
- Put 1 banana in the freezer!

WEEK 3 MENUS

DAY 1

Breakfast:

H$_2$Ox2
Coffee or green tea
Skinny Latkes (page 44)

Morning Snack:

H$_2$Ox2
Espresso Smoothie (page 164) with berries

Lunch:

H_2Ox2

Coffee, tea, or seltzer water

Veggie Carbonara (page 68)

Afternoon Snack:

H_2Ox2

Apple with Almond Butter (page 165)

Dinner:

H_2Ox2

Seltzer water

Pork Loin with Braised Collard Greens (page 117)

DAY 2

Breakfast:

H_2Ox2

Coffee or green tea

Blueberry Muffins (page 51)

Morning Snack:

H_2Ox2

Apple with Almond Butter (page 165)

Lunch:

H_2Ox2

Coffee, tea, or seltzer water

Roasted Eggplant Salad (page 97)

Afternoon Snack:

H_2Ox2
Smashed Pea "Guac" (page 161)

Dinner:

H_2Ox2
Seltzer water
Blackened Mahi Mahi with Fennel Slaw (page 127)

DAY 3

Breakfast:

H_2Ox2
Coffee or green tea
Breakfast Burrito Bowl (page 56)

Morning Snack:

H_2Ox2
Greek Yogurt with Berries (page 162)

Lunch:

H_2Ox2
Coffee, tea, or seltzer water
Beef Chili (page 76)

Afternoon Snack:

H_2Ox2
Turkey Rolls (page 167) with an apple

Dinner:

H$_2$Ox2

Seltzer water

Banh Mi Chicken Salad (page 99)

DAY 4—MEATLESS

Breakfast:

H$_2$Ox2

Coffee or green tea

Apple Pie Shake (page 32)

Morning Snack:

H$_2$Ox2

Apple with Almond Butter (page 165)

Lunch:

H$_2$Ox2

Coffee, tea, or seltzer water

Tempeh Burrito (page 79)

Afternoon Snack:

H$_2$Ox2

Spiced Almonds (page 158)

Dinner:

H$_2$Ox2

Seltzer water

Colorful Stir-Fry (made with beans) (page 132)

DAY 5

Breakfast:

H_2Ox2

Coffee or green tea

Blueberry Muffins (page 51)

Morning Snack:

H_2Ox2

Apple with Almond Butter (page 165)

Lunch:

H_2Ox2

Coffee, tea, or seltzer water

Irish Flag Flying (page 89)

Afternoon Snack:

H_2Ox2

Balsamic Cottage Cheese (page 166) with peppers or berries

Dinner:

H_2Ox2

Seltzer water

Lemon Garlic Goodness Soup (page 129)

DAY 6

Breakfast:

H_2Ox2

Coffee or green tea

Sweet Potato Baked Eggs (page 52)

Morning Snack:

H$_2$Ox2

Espresso Smoothie (page 164) with berries

Lunch:

H$_2$Ox2

Coffee, tea, or seltzer water

New Mexican Quinoa Salad (page 72)

Afternoon Snack:

H$_2$Ox2

Apple with Almond Butter (page 165) and a side of berries

Dinner:

H$_2$Ox2

Seltzer water

Chicken Romana (page 137)

DAY 7

Breakfast:

H$_2$Ox2

Coffee or green tea

Power Wrap (page 58) with a side of berries

Morning Snack:

H$_2$Ox2

Spiced Almonds (page 158)

Lunch:

H$_2$Ox2

Coffee, tea, or seltzer water

Spanish Salad with Cucumber Pico de Gallo (page 82)

Afternoon Snack:

H$_2$Ox2

Apple with Almond Butter (page 165)

Dinner:

H$_2$Ox2

Seltzer water

French Halibut with Green Beans (page 152)

WEEK 4

Produce Section Shopping List

Fruit

7 apples

3 or 4 pints fresh berries

1 kiwi

1 pear

1 peach

2 avocados

4 lemons

3 limes

2 bananas

Vegetables

1 sweet potato

1 bag of spinach

1 bunch of kale

2 bunches of Swiss chard

1 bunch/bag of arugula

1 yellow squash

1 zucchini

1 large head of broccoli (or 1 bag of florets)

1 small head of cauliflower (or 1 bag of florets)

6 red bell peppers

12 plum tomatoes

1 pint cherry tomatoes

7 to 10 Persian cucumbers

1 bunch of scallions

1 small bunch of asparagus

1 package of crimini mushrooms (about 15 mushrooms)

1 butternut squash

1 spaghetti squash

1 head of red cabbage

1 head of Bibb or Boston lettuce

1 handful of green beans

2 celery stalks

1 beet

Fresh Herbs

Basil

Parsley

Mint

Oregano

Thyme

Cilantro

Eggs/Dairy Section Shopping List

8 single-serving containers of plain nonfat Greek yogurt

2 single-serving containers of plain 2% fat Greek yogurt

2 to 4 single-serving containers of low-fat cottage cheese

1 small container of feta cheese (if you don't have any left over from last week)

1 dozen omega-3 eggs

Meat/Seafood Section Shopping List

4 ounces wild salmon

4 ounces large shrimp

7 boneless, skinless chicken breasts

8 ounces lean round steak (have the butcher cut it into two 4-ounce portions)

4 ounces sliced low-sodium deli turkey

Miscellaneous Items Shopping List

Oil-packed sun-dried tomatoes

Almond milk

Almond meal

DO-AHEAD DETAILS

- Make 2 batches of My Signature No-Oil Hummus (page 67) and store in an airtight container in the fridge.
- Make 1 batch of Guacamole (page 56) and store in an airtight container in the fridge.
- Make 1 batch of Pico de Gallo (page 45) and store in an airtight container in the fridge.
- Make 1 batch of Spiced Almonds (page 158) and store in a sealed plastic bag.
- Oven-roast 4 boneless, skinless chicken breasts and store in an airtight container in the fridge.
- Roast 2 plum tomatoes (see sidebar on page 156) and store in an airtight container in the fridge.
- Put 2 bananas in the freezer!

WEEK 4 MENUS

DAY 1

Breakfast:

H$_2$Ox2

Coffee or green tea

Overloaded Baked Potato (page 46)

Morning Snack:

H_2Ox2

Greek Yogurt with Mixed Berries (page 162)

Lunch:

H_2Ox2

Coffee, tea, or seltzer water

Beet Tabbouleh (page 83)

Afternoon Snack:

H_2Ox2

Apple with Almond Butter (page 165) and a side of berries

Dinner:

H_2Ox2

Seltzer water

Beef Stew over Cauliflower "Couscous" (page 112)

DAY 2—MEATLESS

Breakfast:

H_2Ox2

Coffee or green tea

Quinoa Cakes (page 41)

Morning Snack:

H_2Ox2

My Signature No-Oil Hummus (page 67) with veggies

Lunch:

H$_2$Ox2
Coffee, tea, or seltzer water
Garbanzo Falafel Salad (page 81)

Afternoon Snack:

H$_2$Ox2
Spiced Almonds (page 158) and an apple

Dinner:

H$_2$Ox2
Seltzer water
Sesame Bowl (page 98)

DAY 3

Breakfast:

H$_2$Ox2
Coffee or green tea
Overloaded Toast (page 37)

Morning Snack:

H$_2$Ox2
Smashed Pea "Guac" (page 161)

Lunch:

H$_2$Ox2
Coffee, tea, or seltzer water
Sesame Bowl (page 98)

Afternoon Snack:

H_2Ox2

Apple with Almond Butter (page 165)

Dinner:

H_2Ox2

Seltzer water

Steak and Warm Spinach Salad (page 136)

DAY 4

Breakfast:

H_2Ox2

Coffee or green tea

Apple Pie Shake (page 32)

Morning Snack:

H_2Ox2

Espresso Smoothie (page 164) with berries

Lunch:

H_2Ox2

Coffee, tea, or seltzer water

Harpersized Salad (page 94)

Afternoon Snack:

H_2Ox2

Roasted Tomato and Basil Hummus (page 156)

Dinner:

H$_2$Ox2
Seltzer water
Baked Squash (page 123)

DAY 5

Breakfast:

H$_2$Ox2
Coffee or green tea
Breakfast Burrito Bowl (page 56)

Morning Snack:

H$_2$Ox2
Apple with Almond Butter (page 165)

Lunch:

H$_2$Ox2
Coffee, tea, or seltzer water
Greens Minestrone Soup (page 105)

Afternoon Snack:

H$_2$Ox2
Greek Yogurt with Mixed Berries (page 162)

Dinner:

H$_2$Ox2
Seltzer water
Chimichurri Steak (page 146)

Breakfast:

H₂Ox2
Coffee or green tea
Peachy Keen Smoothie (page 35)

Morning Snack:

H₂Ox2
Apple with Almond Butter (page 165)

Lunch:

H₂Ox2
Coffee, tea, or seltzer water
Lemon-Basil Chicken Salad (page 103)

Afternoon Snack:

H₂Ox2
Turkey Rolls (page 167) with a side of berries

Dinner:

H₂Ox2
Seltzer water
Creole Shrimp (page 149)

DAY 7

Breakfast:

H₂Ox2
Coffee or green tea
Spicy Green Shake (page 33)

Morning Snack:

H_2Ox2
Balsamic Cottage Cheese (page 166) with mixed berries

Lunch:

H_2Ox2
Coffee, tea, or seltzer water
Salmon Tacos with Avocado Crema (page 90)

Afternoon Snack:

H_2Ox2
Apple with Almond Butter (page 165)

Dinner:

H_2Ox2
Seltzer water
Almond-Crusted Chicken with Balsamic Green Beans (page 151)

ACKNOWLEDGMENTS

First and foremost, I want to thank Danielle Bernabe for her fantastic taste buds and for her dedication in helping me with the recipes in this book. Thank you to Marnie Cochran and the team at Ballantine for believing in me and in my passion for a healthier future. And, of course, thank you to my team—Brett Hansen, Richard Abate and P.J. Shapiro, and Nicole Trinler— for their continuous support and hard work.

INDEX

BOB HARPER is a world-renowned fitness expert and the longest-reigning star of the NBC reality series *The Biggest Loser,* which finished a fifteenth season in 2014. He has released several popular fitness DVDs and is the author of the number one *New York Times* bestselling books *The Skinny Rules* and *Jumpstart to Skinny.* Harper lives in Los Angeles with his dog, Karl.

WWW.MYTRAINERBOB.COM

THE **SKINNY MEALS**
RESTOCK YOUR PANTRY
SHOPPING LIST

DRINKS

Herbal tea

Coffee or espresso

Seltzer water

Protein powder (egg protein powder or whey protein isolate)

COOKING OILS, VINEGARS, CONDIMENTS, AND PICKLED THINGS

Olive oil (and an olive oil mister so that you can control the amount you use in cooking)

Toasted sesame oil

Coconut oil

Bragg Liquid Aminos

Agave syrup

Good-quality balsamic vinegar—red or white, or both

Red wine vinegar

Apple cider vinegar

Worcestershire sauce

Tabasco sauce

Sriracha hot sauce

Capers

Black olives (canned or fresh, pitted)

Green olives (canned or fresh, pitted)

Small cans of chipotle chiles in adobo sauce

Dijon mustard

BAKING AISLE INGREDIENTS

New containers of your favorite dried herbs: basil, bay leaf, cayenne pepper, chili powder, cinnamon, cumin, curry powder, garlic powder, ginger, herbes de Provence, onion powder, oregano, rosemary, tarragon, thyme

Vanilla extract

Baking powder

Baking soda

Rolled oats

Ground flaxseed (be sure to store this in your fridge)

DAIRY AND CHEESE

Unsweetened almond milk

Block of parmesan cheese

CANNED GOODS

Cans or packets of water-packed tuna

Low-sodium canned beans—white (cannellini), black, garbanzo and kidney beans

Low-sodium chicken and vegetable broth

Low-sodium canned crushed tomatoes

Tomato paste

NUTS AND SEEDS

Pre-portioned packets of raw or dry-roasted almonds

Almond butter or all-natural peanut butter (no sugar added)

Walnuts

Cashews (unsalted, raw)

Pine nuts

Unsalted pepitas (pumpkin seeds)

(cut this page out and post where you'll see it daily)

GRAINS AND PASTA

Whole-grain pasta—pick any shape you like

Quinoa

Farro

Lentils

Brown rice (individual precooked packages are the best for portion control)

AROMATICS

Yellow onions

Red onions

Shallots

Several bulbs of garlic

Ginger root

Restock Your Refrigerator (Weekly)

A dozen eggs (those with added omega-3s are best)

Lean ground turkey

Boneless, skinless chicken breasts

Fish fillets (wrap separately and store in the freezer if you're not going to eat within two days)

Tempeh

Low-sodium sliced turkey breast

6-ounce containers of plain nonfat Greek yogurt

Small containers of low-fat cottage cheese

Avocados

Apples

Berries—fresh or frozen (with no added fruit juice or sugars)

Cucumbers (Persian)

Lemons, limes, and oranges (for use in many recipes and to flavor your water)

Sweet potatoes

Mixed salad greens

Spinach and kale and any vegetables you want to try—either in your main meals or for snack time (see page 17 for my list of "As Much as You Want, Anytime Veggies")

Tomatoes

Fresh herbs (parsley, basil, and cilantro show up in many of my recipes)